Emma Bridgewater

PATTERN

Emma Bridgewater

PATTERN

Photography by Andrew Montgomery

SALT · YARD
BOOK C°

Introduction

When I set about creating a range of kitchen pottery made in Stoke-on-Trent thirty years ago my mind was teeming with ideas for the shapes; I had a burgeoning plan for the technique I planned to master, for the decoration of these functional wares; and I simply assumed that I would have no trouble producing as many patterns as I needed to make each season fly. It's such a strange feeling, looking back and realising just how utterly unready I was for what lay ahead. But ignorance, enthusiasm and huge energy, coupled with a very pressing need to generate an income for myself, all combined with the input of a procession of people who have worked with me over the years to turn my plans into reality. Emma Bridgewater shapes are distinctive, and I'm proud of them, and I continue to add to the range steadily, but the demand for a stream – no, a river! – of new surface designs is an unavoidable, undodgeable commercial reality. And I think that maybe I would have failed this challenge dramatically, dismally, if Matthew had not appeared, tanned, sockless, in tennis shoes and a slightly stained but definitely stylish double-breasted suit, down the aisle of the trade fair where I was accustomed to showing each new collection.

That was a gift fair called Top Drawer, which at the time was held in the old Derry & Toms building in Kensington High Street. It was itself a new venture, creative and informal; it provided a springboard for a number of start-ups in the early 1980s and the organisers were very kind to me. My stand was always noisy and busy, as my instinct was to throw a party, so there was always plenty to eat and drink, and customers often had to fight their way in through my enthusiastic friends and family, there in hordes to provide moral support. Matt liked the look of me, and my business, and he laid siege. My assistant Antonia immediately spotted that he was *the one*, and she arranged with him that I'd meet him for lunch at the Chelsea Arts Club. It went well, she was right, and we were married ten months later.

We didn't immediately throw in our lots together as far as work was concerned. We waited a further eighteen months before we started working with one another, but since then it has been shoulder to shoulder all the way. As a trained designer, a really good painter and illustrator, and an unbelievably prolific worker, Matthew has been a vast creative powerhouse in the company. And to cap these formidable contributions, since 2008 he has run the company. This is all by way of explaining why I have dwelt heavily (but not exclusively) in this book on the hand-printed patterns known as spongeware, which are mostly my work.

But that's as may be – Matthew and I work closely together, and we interfere ceaselessly in each other's ideas, never hesitating to proffer unsolicited advice, despite having worked out that there is nothing less welcome in one's working life; so it's often hard to say exactly who did what, who thought of this or that detail. But as a rule of thumb, spongeware is liberating for me in the same degree that it is constraining for him. The thing about printing a pattern using a piece of sponge cut into a simple shape is that less really is more – a subtle or detailed design can very easily look fussy, and lack impact. By the same token a struggling draughtsman such as myself has to think hard, eliminate complexity, and push for simple and punchy effect, and the technique suits these traits. Matt says that I think out a design while he draws one out, and I think that's about right.

The look of my early trade fair stands was created by using deep-coloured photographer's paper to line the booth, bringing a rug from home to cover the nylon carpet provided, filling galvanised buckets with whole trays of flowers from Covent Garden Market. But the key was Margaret Martin's ingenious shelving system. She made me two sets of step-ladders, with shelves that slotted onto the steps and bolted together in the corner for stability. She is a genius.

In planning this book I sat down to look back over the company's history of design. That pointed out the first challenge – the design archive can still only be described as a work in progress. We have always focused upon the present; we have kept scanty records and, in the early years at least, a very thin and somewhat random selection of samples of past designs. The back catalogues are helpful, and I have frequently felt extremely grateful to Steven Jenkins for the hard work that he put into chronicling the company from its inception up to 2006. But there was no master list of all Emma Bridgewater designs, and until 2000, no digital records of any of the products. Because of course, for the first ten years there were no computers anywhere in the business; everything was on paper, and such records as survive are often scattered and tattered ... So you may picture me, busy with lists and lists, and lists of lists, feeling fairly challenged by my self-appointed task of creating a worthwhile and telling overview of Emma Bridgewater designs from the early years to the present day.

In order to illustrate them, we have had to recreate from scratch the majority of the patterns referenced here. Once I actually had a list of all the Emma Bridgewater patterns in existence, I realised that I had to make a selection, for fear of a major overload. So I tried out various selection principles, and what came through was a clarifying decision: I would chronicle a completely personal selection. I chose my personal favourites, spotting the designs which come with stories worth telling. Many of the patterns really are more Matt's than mine, and to write about them well, I would need his collaboration, so I have not included, for example, the Birds range, as it is so completely based on his knowledge and his love and feelings for British birds.

But stop. I know that lots of people read my name, scratch about in their minds, draw a memory blank and wonder, slightly crossly, why they are apparently supposed to know anything about Emma Bridgewater. This often happens, trust me. There I am at a party, and I'm introduced by a kind enthusiastic hostess to a fellow guest as 'a famous potter'. I share his mild embarrassment, and in hopes of a swift subject change to best recent read, or great terriers he has known – anything! I will murmur apologetically that I am really *not* a potter, that I am a grubby industrialist, with a factory making useful everyday wares – perhaps he can picture a cosy mug decorated with chickens? Or evocative words about food? He is restless, no gleam of recognition, until I say that our best-seller is a design of colourful polka dots. And the light gratefully dawns. Quite often. And when it doesn't, I'm more than happy to learn his martini recipe, and see him as proof that we still have exciting numbers of new customers to secure, let alone convert ...

I am pretty sure that Polka Dots has been our best-selling design; certainly it has been very popular – and very widely ripped off, too. This is usually a sure sign that a product has achieved recognition, for a surprisingly huge proportion of companies, especially the large retailers, are unabashed about taking a strong idea from a small company and, having made some minor changes, selling it as 'the original'. It can be a bit annoying.

So before I go any further, let me tell you, by way of an introduction to my company and to this book (for you should know that this is a flavour of what's to come in the rest of it), how Polka Dots came into being.

When my children were starting out at their various primary schools, and tackling the mysterious process that is learning to read, I instinctively reached for the books that I remembered as being the ur-texts from my own childhood, and also influential in the lives of my younger siblings. First up is, without hesitation, Beatrix Potter, whose compelling and stimulating prose is my literary gold; also Maurice Sendak – his *Little Bear* books, which preceded *Where the Wild Things Are*, make a whole world, with a very simple collection of words. Miffy, Tintin, Johnny Crow, the Velveteen Rabbit, the Flower Fairies and Ameliaranne Stiggins were just a few of the characters

I bonded with from the books that Mum read out loud to me, encouraged me to read on my own and that I read out loud to my little sisters and then to my own children. I never really seem to have stopped reading them; I took *The Tailor of Gloucester* with me often when I went to see Mum, when she was in a coma in hospital, to keep us both safe, to have something good to read to her.

But I had forgotten all about the utter joy of Ladybird books – that is, until Worstead Village School had a clear-out and de-acquisitioned most of its library, including its huge collection of Ladybirds, in favour of I.T. (don't start me ...). I bought them all for a song, and pretty much rolled about in them in a nostalgic trance of lemon-yellow party dresses, shopping baskets, school caps, autumn landscapes, battles, shipwrecks and coal miners. The especially evocative pictures in *The Party* and *Shopping with Mother* are by Harry Wingfield. I love his world. John Berry is another favourite Ladybird illustrator; for example, *The Farm* has his loving and information-packed illustrations. These books are simple, so simple: they condense a great life into an easy illustrated essay, an account of an industry into a narrative which is readily accessible to a seven-year-old; the experience of a shopping trip, starting at a new school, or a birthday party are conveyed in a tight vocabulary for early reading success, but most of all they have a powerful atmosphere. When I rediscovered them I was back in the room with my four-/five-/six-/seven-/eight-year-old self, and I could almost smell what it felt like to realise that I could read, followed swiftly by the thrill of understanding that reading captured feelings. I was a madeleine, and the slightly murky, pasty, pastel-colour palette of *Shopping with Mother* last seen by me in 1965 was a whole bath of lime blossom tea in which I bathed until I almost melted.

And when I calmed down, I was still in the grip of a strong desire to bring back that time of my early childhood, to conjure up its atmosphere in pattern: Polka Dots was (eventually, tangentially) the result. The components of the look I was longing for were varied: around the time that my son Michael was born, in 1999, I accelerated my collecting passion for late 50s and early 60s Staffordshire pottery, then one Monday in Aylsham market the melamine and plastic-covered furniture in the lowliest furniture barn struck me as totally covetable, along with charity shop hauls of pale Paisley eiderdowns, crocheted bedspreads and a cocoon of cosy familiar stuff surrounded with which I would find a way back to 1965, to the years, the atmosphere, of my early childhood. From about this time our catalogue shoots were often styled with these nostalgic things as props.

Meanwhile the Conran Shop commissioned some exclusive designs, way back in 1990, which hung in there for ages – simple Stars and Polos in classic cobalt blue; then, for some designs by Mary Fedden in 2000 and 2001, we added a handful of new colours to our range – and these two strands fused one day, when I asked Helen in the factory studio to try out some simple graphic designs, scattering a single motif as for the Conran Blue Stars, trying out some of the new colours. She came up with a mug (which incidentally bore the legend 'Happy Birthday'), surrounded with fingerprint-sized polka dots in pale green, deep red, dark green, tawny yellow and lavender.

To give our stand at Birmingham a suitably retro
look for promoting Polka Dots I pursued my interest in
the look of Marmoleum lino to its inevitable conclusion
and had dinner-plate sized polka dots cut out in five colours
approximately matched to the polka dot colours set
in a cream floor: the result was very pleasing,
I can't think why I've never done it at home.

Her choice of colours was instantly just right and the birthday message pointed to the inherent strength of the simple decoration – what it simply sang out was PARTY. This pattern alone can make a festive atmosphere: I later lent 400 Polka Dot plates to some friends, whose tables bore just white paper cloths with bunches of wild flowers in jam jars – the look was perfect. The following season we put Polka Dots, no added message required, on to a small range of shapes, and the success of the pattern was sealed. Since 2002 I estimate that we have sold something like two million pieces of Polka Dot pottery, across almost every Emma Bridgewater shape, with many messages, in different colour combinations, and alongside a changing cast of coordinating designs such as Hearts, Stripes, Fireworks and more recently Folk Border. Polka Dot Pumpkins is not my favourite pattern, but I love that the concept translates into a beautiful special of scattered cockerels for Howden's Joinery, or some years ago a design for Polos and Polka Dots for Rachel's Dairy.

A SUITABLY RETRO PARTY RECIPE
CORONATION CHICKEN

Serves 8

To poach the chicken

1 x 2kg free-range chicken | 2 celery sticks, halved
1 carrot, roughly sliced | $\frac{1}{2}$ large onion, sliced
6 black peppercorns | 2 fresh bay leaves
Salt and freshly ground black pepper

For the curried mayonnaise

2 tablespoons sunflower oil | 1 small onion, finely chopped
1 tablespoon mild curry powder | $\frac{1}{2}$ teaspoon ground coriander
1 teaspoon ground turmeric | $\frac{1}{2}$ teaspoon freshly grated nutmeg
$\frac{1}{2}$ teaspoon ground cinnamon | $\frac{1}{2}$ teaspoon cayenne pepper
$\frac{1}{2}$ teaspoon paprika powder | 2 tablespoons apricot jam
125g mango chutney | 200ml mayonnaise
200ml crème fraîche

For the rice salad

300g long-grain rice | 200g piece of cucumber
200g frozen petit pois, thawed | 1 tablespoon white wine vinegar
$\frac{1}{4}$ teaspoon Dijon mustard | 4 tablespoons extra virgin olive oil

To finish

4 dried apricots, thinly sliced across | 25g toasted flaked almonds

Put the whole chicken into a large pan with the rest of the poaching ingredients and 1 teaspoon of salt and cover with cold water. Bring to the boil, then cover and simmer for 45 minutes, or until when you break the leg away from the main body, the meat is white and firm with no traces of pink left. Turn off the heat and leave the chicken to cool in the liquid. It will carry on cooking as it is cooling.

For the curried mayonnaise, heat the sunflower oil in a small pan, add the chopped onion, cover and cook very gently for 10 minutes until soft and translucent. Add the spices and cook gently for another 5 minutes. Add the jam and mango chutney and cook on a low heat until everything has melted together. Leave to cool, then blend in a mini food processor until smooth. Tip the mixture into a large mixing bowl and stir in the mayonnaise and crème fraîche. Season to taste with salt and a little pepper.

Cook the rice in a pan of boiling salted water for 12 minutes or until cooked but still firm to the bite. Drain, rinse with cold water and leave to cool.

Cut the cucumber into small dice, about the same size as the peas. Tip the rice into a bowl and stir in the cucumber and peas. Whisk the vinegar, mustard, olive oil and some seasoning together to make a dressing and stir it through the rice salad.

Remove the chicken from the liquid and remove the meat from the bones, discarding the skin. Shred the meat and stir it into the curried mayonnaise. (Do not discard the cooking liquid. It can be chilled or frozen and used as a base for delicious soups and casseroles or to cook pasta in.)

Spoon the rice salad around the edge of a large serving platter and put the chicken mixture in the centre. Garnish with the dried apricots and toasted flaked almonds and serve.

FLOWERS

One of the very best ways to appreciate flowers is from a car. On neglected roundabouts, on verges all over the country, by the windiest of lanes or a whizzing dual carriageway, and even on the embankments of the motorway, you will see how carelessly, abundantly, beautifully and with no planning at all the wild flowers of England fling themselves about, star the mown grass, tangle the hedges, and most especially how they lavish themselves in utterly perfect ever-changing versions of the best ever herbaceous borders. Of course, the councils and authorities are always intervening, sometimes with benign effects, I will concede, but more frequently with disastrously destructive mowing programmes – for example, slap in the middle of the nesting season, just so that we can all speed slightly more foolishly on to the next thing.

I know that the motorway embankments are not *au naturel*, they are strimmed, and also their trees are cut down in swathes just as they come to maturity lest health and safety guidelines might be breached. I am aware of successful municipal planting schemes along our roads – in Norwich the splashes and pools of the crocuses between the carriageways of the ring road in February are an especial pleasure. But notwithstanding these interferences, the wild flowers burst out – they recall the lost bucolic past and they grab their chances wherever the soil is turned over; they redeem the heartlessness of how we live with their boundless grace and loveliness. They constantly heal and restore the land, and make it beautiful.

I was aware of this all over again recently when I had a blow-out on the M25 on the way to my father's wedding. The event was, as a puncture at speed is bound to be, rather rattling, and as I bundled out of the passenger door and clambered inelegantly over the crash barrier, with huge lorries thundering past in speedy succession, I felt shaky. While I waited for the AA, I walked up and down to keep warm, and soon realised that what I had taken for early flowering oilseed rape, self-seeding in the grass on the bank below me, was in fact a sheet of cowslips coming into flower. I picked a small bunch, marvelling at the slender beauty of these plants, once so plentiful, now quite rare, growing strongly among the roadside litter of cans, bottles and fast-food wrappers. And I realised that now I felt calm, separate for a while from the stress of cars and motorways and burst tyres.

When you look, these treats are widespread, everywhere: Matthew spotted a bank of brightest pink orchids beside a busy road in Oxfordshire; and between Worstead and North Walsham the natural succession of wild flowers on the verges produces in May a bounty of moon daisies as romantic and dreamlike as any director of a shampoo commercial could possibly wish to find or contrive for his models to skip about in.

Our gardening efforts to capture for ourselves some of this lavish wonder are, I always feel, poignant at heart, in that they unconsciously show the gulf that lies between our contrivances and the mighty power of the natural world. I love that we struggle on in our efforts to capture and crystallise the beauty of flowers, no matter how inadequate the results – on curtains for caravans and carpets in castles; on summer dresses for skinny young girls or covers for fat comfy sofas; on bathroom tiles and on packaging of all descriptions, from soap to loo cleaner. I am moved by the Islamic belief that the task is so impossible (that is, the challenge of adequately representing the work of the hand of the great creator) that it is sacrilege to make the attempt. But I much prefer our own Christian tradition, because I believe that it's better by far to try and fail, and in so doing glimpse the discrepancy, than to be forbidden the attempt.

Chintz

This was a very early pattern, which scrambled into my head fully formed while I was still absorbed in the challenges of cutting out the sponges with which to print my first mugs and jugs. My boyfriend Alex had a breakthrough one day in 1985, while we were still struggling to find natural sponges which retained just enough of their stumpy, denser root so that we could raze a flat surface, barely a couple of centimetres in diameter, into which, using scalpels and nail scissors, we might laboriously cut a simple motif, and thus create a printing tool.

I squeezed and studied natural sponges in expensive chemists and wondered if I should go to Turkey to try to collect the roots of these sponges, presumably on the quays or beaches where the boats landed them, and the fishermen trimmed off and discarded the stems to make a nice round soft pouffe. More practical, Alex's mind moved along to consider unnatural (by which I mean artificial) sponges, so much more readily available, whose very feel set my teeth on edge. This was an aversion I had to get over; I have been handling chemical foam ever since, with all its associations of toxic black smoke, cheap furniture and general bedsit-ness. Alex managed to find, doubtless in one of the endlessly productive railway-arch-based businesses locally in Brixton, a couple of square cushions of furnishing foam. These had been cured (cooked, basically) in a mould, giving a useful, slightly crisp, flat but slightly textured, even surface on to which we could draw a simple shape. Next, using an electrician's small soldering iron (I have written elsewhere about how practical Alex is; he is good at solving physical problems), we carved out the design – melting or cutting away the unwanted spaces, after which, as the printing block emerged, we tidied the result with nail scissors.

This new home-made technology changed the game: I could see how we could now reliably source the necessary supplies as we got busier and the decorating girls needed a regular supply of sponges. Better still, I need no longer confine myself to making designs out of motifs no bigger than two centimetres across.

As I grappled with my emerging ideas about the pottery – its shapes and their decoration – I swiftly set about clarifying my tastes, and seeking out collections and individual pieces of old wares to broaden my knowledge. I knew the relevant ceramics collections in all the obvious museums pretty much by heart – the V & A in South Ken, the Fitzwilliam in Cambridge, the Ashmolean in Oxford – but ceramics curators have very little interest in the sort of everyday pottery I had in mind, which instead lay in the hands of dealers, who so often had 'a lovely one like that, but I sold it just last week', and private collectors – some of them like my mother, who used and broke the pieces I remembered, often before I got there to draw them. I made friends with Richard Scott in Holt, and Constance Stobo off Kensington Church Street. The Lacquer Chest, in the same part of London, was a treasure trove, as were Stephen Long on Stamford Bridge, and Robert and Josyane Young in Battersea. I was diverted when I discovered Rogers de Rijn, a beautiful shop in Chelsea, full of Wemyss ware, whose exuberant hand-painted Edwardian flowers completely gripped my imagination – how might I make something like this? And using Alex's new artificial sponge I saw that size was no longer a limiting factor; now I could cut sponges as large as I could hold. Moreover, I realised that while I was using old spongeware as my inspiration, I no longer had to replicate its repeating border designs – I was free! Now I saw that I could print big soft, splashy pink roses all over my pottery, something like Wemyss: Chintz was the result.

In the mid 1980s the China Collection in the V & A was almost abandoned; on winter afternoons I would have it all to myself for hours. The wind howled in the roof as I drew shapes and made notes. I adore its refurbished incarnation, but can't help missing the solitude it used to offer.

All the early samples, including the first dish printed with Chintz, were decorated in Brixton, at Alex's kitchen table, trying out lots of new sponges, using underglaze stains, ground up on a tile with a palette knife and wetted to a paste as instructed by the staff at Potterycrafts in Battersea. The results were variable, but shared a looseness, a softness and a texture which it has been impossible to preserve intact as the business has grown. The colours we work with now are of course commercially developed, and for sound safety reasons the heavy metal components are increasingly restricted, which is as it should be; and also, there is a desire for consistency between batches so that a replacement saucer closely matches its cup. All these developments are basically positive, but I do miss the watery gentleness, and the variations of the early colours, and most particularly in this pattern whose charm depends on an impressionistic handling which is at odds with producing ever larger batches.

Roses are perhaps the first and last flower I would name to conjure the magic of English flowers both wild and cultivated: their infinite variety embraces all tastes, from obedient suburban hybrid teas (so loveless on their erect bushes, so delicious in enormous jugfuls), to thorny burglar-repelling devils disguised as clouds of sweetness, or prim miniatures in swan-shaped patio pots, huge climbers rampaging into the treetops, modest ramblers to scent a cottage porch or a wreath of innocent white dog roses fit for Tess Durbeyfield. Chintz was the star of my very first proper catalogue, and with an old friend, Harry Cory Wright, taking the photographs, I worked all out to find a way to imbue the pottery with romance. Harry is a genius, and the battered old barns, full of broken furniture, old garden tools and forgotten pictures at his house in Norfolk provided the perfect setting.

Harry's early pictures had potting-shed romance. I think they are effective because all types of garden sheds, weirdly even the brand new empty ones in the garden centre, work a powerful spell, redolent of battered equipment for secret projects, of last summer and its games of croquet, and of secluded tree-screened places to hide away. All my life I have been in thrall to romance; I long to conjure that fragile magic which inspires dreams, breeds creativity, flashes beauty into new places and makes an ordinary day suddenly wonderful.

> For me Oxford is the perfect city, with its ancient university, beautiful secretive colleges and its two rivers, with many beautiful water meadows along their banks. It has everything going for it, but I could see that it was foolish not to provide much more gardening scope on which to unleash Matthew's amazing energy.

When in 2009 we moved to Jericho in Oxford, only a few streets away from the house I grew up in, I was entirely happy in the company of ghosts from my childhood, so wrapped up was I in the fact that I was walking the very same pavements which were cut through with the same drainage brick entries to each house, with their specific feel of squares of white chocolate, that I sometimes had to think hard for a moment to remember that I was out with Michael, and who Michael was, so sure was I that I was ten years old myself and going out roller-skating with Vicky and Choss. But obviously the rest of the family didn't share these memories, and they were in one way or another restless in the city, longing for space, for opportunities to plant many trees or to make a kitchen garden; they itched for wilder fishing and wider horizons.

So I went house-hunting around the villages outside the city. I was not sure what I was looking for, but that never worried me; I just felt that I'd know it when I saw it. In the end it wasn't me who discovered Bampton, but

the handsome, tall and loping estate agent from Summertown, who called me one day and said, 'I've found it,' leaving little room for doubt. I sometimes like being told what to do, so I arranged to meet him there on a sunny April afternoon, and he was right. 'It' was an extremely run-down farm, tenanted for centuries and much abused. But the beautiful wraith of romance, maybe now in the guise of a dangerous siren, slipped around the corners ahead of me as we trudged through nettles and docks across sandy expanses of mud, peering into cavernous asbestos barns scurrying with rats and sparrows, with here and there some old barns and stables of stone and brick to relieve the cracked concrete. The house itself was extraordinarily neglected, with only the most basic plumbing and electrics, and much of it chilly to the bone: a nondescript Victorian extension grafted clumsily onto a medieval gate house. But the wraith was waiting, and beckoned us on, up a spiral staircase, into a crudely divided room with breathtaking stone bones of early medieval vaulting. As my daughter Margaret and our friend Ivan continued exploring with the estate agent I stood by a huge stone fireplace, looking out of a filthy gothic window, and realised that I was just as doomed to take this on as I had been when I saw my first derelict pottery in Stoke-on-Trent, because here was romance.

We are deep in the work of excavating the beautiful moated manor buried deep beneath the years of toil and hardship, but from the first, the goal was all too clear. If we succeed, when the work is done, and time has passed again, then if you were to arrive here as a ghostly intruder from the future, when our current labours have been patinated with a little dust and some flattering cobwebs, perhaps the house will be as that wraith described it to me. Before you can climb in through the drawing-room window you will have to push back the tresses of white Seagull roses, and inside, the paper on the walls, faded and stained in places, is an old pattern of pink roses. There is a faint breath of pot-pourri from a cracked lustre bowl on the piano. As you wander from room to room you will find only dogs sleeping on tapestry-hung beds, vaulted ceilings, bathrooms with brass taps and huge cast-iron baths on lion feet, a blue print of wild roses in the huge washbasins, and rosy-coloured pamments underfoot. If you let yourself out of the back door, you will leave through the kitchen garden, under rose arches, then through an orchard and back down the drive, over the water, down a lime avenue and back to your car, where you will lean for a moment, wondering if you have just walked into a dream. A dream full of ghosts and roses.

25

TRIFLE WITH ROSE PETALS

If possible this is strewn with the heavenly-smelling petals of
Rosa pimpinellifolia William III, but any pink rose petals will do.

Serves 8

Approx. 12 sponge fingers
6–8 tablespoons Marsala, Madeira or medium sweet sherry

For the fresh raspberry jelly
200g caster sugar | 500g fresh raspberries | 9 small sheets of leaf gelatine

For the custard
300ml full cream milk | 300ml double cream
1 vanilla pod, split open lengthways | 6 large free-range egg yolks
3 tablespoons caster sugar | 3 tablespoons cornflour

To finish
300ml double cream | Fresh, pale pink rose petals

Line the base of your trifle bowl (one that is about 18cm across and 12cm deep)
with the sponge fingers and drizzle with the Marsala, Madeira or sherry.

To make the jelly, put 750ml of cold water and the caster sugar into a
pan and stir over a low heat until the sugar has dissolved. Add 200g of the
raspberries, bring back to a simmer, then take off the heat. Tip into a food
processor and blend together, then rub through a sieve to remove the seeds.
Return the juice to the pan and re-warm briefly. Soak the leaves of gelatine in
a separate bowl of tepid water for 5 minutes. Remove the gelatine leaves from
the bowl of water (they will be softened by now), add them to the pan and stir
gently until completely dissolved. Leave until cool, then stir in the remaining
raspberries. Pour the liquid over the sponge fingers, then leave in the fridge
for at least 4 hours, until set.

To make the custard, heat the milk and cream together in a pan with the vanilla
pod. If you can set this aside for a while to infuse, all the better. In a separate bowl,
mix the egg yolks with the caster sugar and cornflour. Bring the milk back up to
the boil, then gradually stir it into the egg yolks, discarding the vanilla pod, and
return to a low heat. Cook gently, stirring, until thickened. Leave to cool.

To assemble the trifle, whip the double cream into soft peaks. Top the jelly
with the custard, then with the whipped cream, and decorate with pink rose
petals (The important thing is that they smell delicious).

Sweet Pea

The very idea of a bunch of sweet pea flowers is so perfectly redolent of early summer, of sweetness and simplicity, that it is no wonder that (young, definitely first-time) brides so often think immediately of sweet pea bouquets, and picture their bridesmaids in sweet pea coloured dresses. They were not a big thing in my mum's gardening repertoire, or not so that I can picture them in any of her various gardens, but I do remember them from my childhood. My friend Clare lived on the farm just over the road from us in Bassingbourn; her Auntie Joan lived in a cottage which we went to often, as it was just across Clare's mum's garden. Everything about Poplar Farm was deeply pleasing to me (despite feeling just slightly nervous of her father and brother, as they were so very rugged and masculine), especially because it was full of a cosy sort of femininity slightly different from that of my mum or stepmother. Clare had lots of older sisters (three of them? Four?), amongst whose collections of *Girl Annuals* and Enid Blyton stories, as well as their left-behind stilettos and foamy party dresses in sweet pea colours, Clare and I played happily for hours on end. Her mum's larder was lined with ranks of her own jams and chutneys, and piled with cake and biscuit tins, filled with home-made delights, ready for us, after school, and for the men when they came in noisily hungry. Clare and I would watch children's telly programmes – *Romper Room*, *Jackanory* or *Crackerjack* – and Clare's mum would wheel in tea on a trolley, which rolled softly on the carpets that were so much woollier than the rush matting and haircord we had at home. But mostly we played outside, where we had a favourite camp in a shepherd's hut which had come to rusty rest in a corner of the big concrete yard.

We designed a collection of furnishing fabrics and wallpapers with Sanderson in 2014 and one of the very nicest and quietest designs is the wallpaper decorated with our Sweet Pea pattern, reversed out in cream on a pale background in several colours.

When we went to visit Auntie Joan she gave us jobs like picking and shelling broad beans, or stripping redcurrants off their stalks and into a Pyrex bowl with a fork, or picking sweet peas in neat bunches. So my first experience was of sweet peas in a gloriously pastel array, with lots of frilly doubles, arranged in careful sprays of an even colour mix – as was firmly ordained by the Women's Institute. These strictures about flower-arranging were not to be breached, as I learned each year when entering posies for the flower-arranging classes at the church fête, where Auntie Joan gave no marks for my

32

childish efforts, and even though I knew she was very fond of me her comments were inflexible: 'no balance' and 'too informal' being her judgements time after time. Her neat, orderly and productive garden had, in spring, rows of crossed bamboos, all regular and firmly tied. She gave us small pairs of scissors to cut the flowers, which we could easily reach from the concrete paths.

I often think, with pleasure and some wistfulness, of Auntie Joan as I pick sweet peas in Matt's kitchen garden; my scissors are always long gone on a grubby, perhaps poultry-related project, and access to the sweet peas is more like an obstacle course, so profuse and full is every inch around his plants. He plants the sweet pea seeds in October and they spend the winter in and out of my airing cupboard, a vital but inevitably aggravating arrangement that makes me predictably annoyed, yet one which I go along with because I adore the results. In the past ten years or so he has concentrated on the variety Matucana, as it is so spectacular that it simply trumps all the rest for its deep purple colour and powerfully wonderful scent. Occasionally one of us weakens and buys a packet or two of a paler variety (whose longer stems are a bit of a bonus), and as Matthew sometimes manages to collect the seed we have outbreaks from time to time of enchanting marbly-streaked sweet peas. The seedlings are repotted using tall pots, so their roots can grow long, then they go out to an unheated greenhouse to toughen up a bit early in the year, until they can be planted around the wigwams, or along the pea-stick rows in March, to flower from April on.

They will continue to flower throughout the summer if we pick the flowers regularly and thoroughly enough to prevent them setting seed. The profusion, the lushness and the sheer wonderfulness of the results frequently provoke disbelief, and frank envy. An old family friend simply stood on the steps of the Wickmere kitchen garden murmuring, 'Oh, f***,' as she surveyed the excesses. What is his secret? I can only say, green fingers. And also dead creatures. The trenches for the sweet peas are double-dug (i.e. deeper than you were thinking), and he lobs into them any chickens recently deceased, meaty kitchen rubbish, guts, etc., after slaughtering a lamb, even roadkill if I'm not in the car to kick up a fuss.

And the result is enough sweet peas to fill containers of all sizes, from little bedside jugs to huge bowls for the table in the hall, which look like great round silky cushions.

Zinnias

A friend, who works as a stylist for a fashion magazine because she has a brilliant eye for what will be next, brought a packet of zinnia seeds back from an American trip about twenty years ago. I really love it when people point you towards a plant you know nothing about – a similar thing happened when Matt's father, Peter, suggested an addition to our herb patch, saying that his mother used to grow summer savory (also known as sarriette) and how delicious it is snipped over boiled new potatoes (which turns out to be true, by the way) – as it's so easy to get in a rut, with gardening as with everything, and to repeat old habits endlessly until your own cooking, or choice of clothes, or indeed your flower beds can almost bore you to sobs.

Jayne's zinnias, initially surprising, provided a wonderful jolt; zinnias come in a rainbow of heavenly zingy, sparky colours, often veering excitingly towards tastelessness; they are an endlessly satisfying component when picking a bunch; the more you cut them the more they flower, and they have an abundant and lengthy season – from late July (June in Matt's polytunnel) right on through October, frosts permitting. Matthew took to them instantly, and he has grown them every year since, without fail, as far as I can remember. But his interest might have waned if we had not seen for ourselves just how varied zinnias can be.

> Matthew insists that it was he who enthused Jayne about zinnias, and not the other way around. We are becoming one of those couples who row on the same subjects enthusiastically, firmly taking up a position, and then merrily adopting the opposing view the next time the subject arises.

Once, as a consolation, following a sentence in the Javits Center (the Summer Gift Show in New York which happens in early September, and where we had a stand for several years, spring and summer – it was purgatorial), we spent two days in the Hamptons. The holiday season was over and the true nature of the place was flowing back into the farms and villages, like the blood supply regained in a cramped limb: homes were being repossessed after lucrative summer letting; their owners, emerging from a summer spent in the garden shed or a daughter's spare room, were now clad in working clothes, hailing each other from pick-ups as they dashed about, consulting with builders and plumbers. The farm stands at the gates were less prinky, but still had produce to sell, and when we stopped at one to buy tomatoes for

our picnic, we were enchanted to see a big bucket of zinnias, some small and star-like, some big as shaggy pompoms on a baby's knitted bonnet, and in a wild array of colours even wider than Jayne's seeds had yielded – from acid green, yellow and cream, through golden to scarlet and shocking pink, and frequently showing the streaky effect caused by the farmer's wife having collected and re-sown her own seeds. The drawback to driving holidays is that you can't reasonably buy more produce than you can eat in today's picnic. With reluctance we forced ourselves not to buy the bucket and its contents, but we were resolved to grow more and more of these exotic gypsies.

SALADE COMPOSÉE

Remember to make a salad of all the delicious tender young veg coming into foaming abundance just as the zinnias blaze into flower. On your very largest meat plate carefully lay a bed of different lettuce leaves, then sprinkle this with several handfuls of peas and beans, shelled, blanched and cooled, some new potatoes, cooled and rolled in a little oil, and some sariette, chopped fine; slice two or three tomatoes, or maybe a couple of handfuls of cherry tomatoes, red, yellow and orange. Soft-boil four fresh eggs, then peel and halve carefully. If there are no vegetarians coming for lunch, you might drape some expensive anchovies across your salad for saline and artistic effect. Dress with your nicest oil, a splash of white wine vinegar, sea salt, black pepper and a very light dusting of sugar, less than half a teaspoon.

When I was thinking about new spongeware designs in 2012 I picked myself a bunch of zinnias in our kitchen garden, and as the sweet peas were looking lovely I mixed the two, went indoors, put the bunch in an old milk bottle and sat down to draw them. I wanted, as always really, to express the particular characteristics of both plants that give me such pleasure. I especially love the way that the centres of the zinnias seem to fill with tiny stars as the flowers reach their peak and move towards setting seed.

There is always a challenge as to how best to convey the wavy delicacies of sweet peas while sidestepping the territories of Georgia O'Keefe, the American painter of huge floral compositions which are just too allusive to sexual parts to look nice on a teapot.

When I had worked on a handful of motifs which I hoped were able to carry my ideas, I made sure that each line drawing was telling, clear and unambiguous. Next, using small tiles made especially for this purpose, I selected the group of colours which best suited my ideas for the effect I wished to make with this new pattern. Then I sent to the factory an email containing the final line drawings for each motif, from which they were to cut this new set of sponges, also the colour instructions, detailing which motifs were to be printed in each colour, and finally, my suggestions as to coverage of each of the shapes I wished to see sampled.

The normal course of events would then be that I would see the fired samples on my next visit to the factory. I might well speak to Leigh, who manages product development, to respond to any of her practical suggestions for improvements, additional samples and any other useful variations. She emails photos to me for commentary to maximise the strength of the first batch of samples in a new design. In this case all went smoothly, and final samples of Zinnias, as the pattern was immediately titled, were readily arrived at. This is not by any means always the case; there are patterns which go backwards and forwards as we juggle dramatic effect with practical application. Roughly speaking, as a designer you often long to use more colours and motifs than the factory can comfortably handle: as a company we need to push ourselves collectively, to improve the skills and speeds of our decorators, producing dramatic, new-looking patterns to catch the imagination of our customers, and at the same time we have to function rationally, to work smart and avoid tying ourselves in production knots – it's a rolling challenge at the heart of the business, and in many ways this is the dynamic that I find the most stimulating and potentially satisfying part of the company, out of all of its functions.

> In the late eighteenth century, Josiah Wedgwood asserted
> his belief that it was pure foolishness to strive to make his
> wares available at lower prices; instead he dedicated himself
> to constant improvement in quality and appeal: oh, I do agree!

I have grown so used to seeing zinnias among Matthew's rows of kale, onions, chard and suchlike that it was a surprise to remember that they have exotic, Mexican origins, and flourish in hot and harsh conditions as well as in our cooler damper gardens. While in Karnatika, in southern India, one February, on an inspired tour led by my indomitable, wonderful cousin Sally, I saw a large bed filled exclusively with zinnias in the garden of Tipu Sultan's beautiful Summer Palace. Most of the people in our group were keen and knowledgeable gardeners, so I was interested that several of them did not recognise these colourful beauties, but I guess that proves that these flowers have recently been a bit out of fashion in Britain.

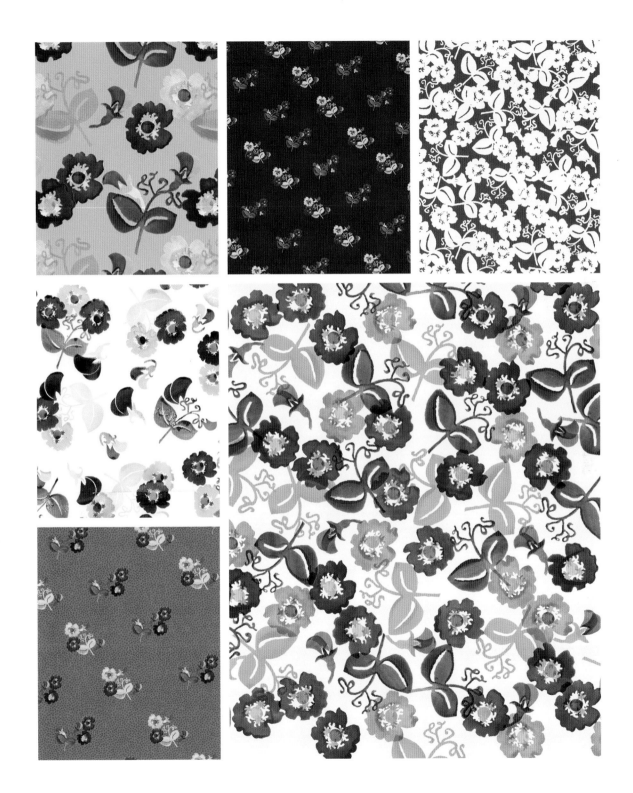

45

I very highly recommend to you this palace. It is built of wood and intricately painted throughout with shameless propaganda for Tipu's (as it was to prove, temporary) supremacy over all foreign interlopers. It contains, amongst other things, a series of beautiful charcoal drawings of his sons by Thomas Hickey, which are especially moving when you learn that they sat for these portraits following the conquest of the nearby fortress of Seringapatam by the army of Sir Arthur Wellesley – later better known as the Duke of Wellington. During the siege Tipu died in fierce hand-to-hand fighting, leaving his sons to be re-educated by the British Raj. Furthermore, the palace is set in beautiful gardens, with an unusual number of huge trees, as well as beds of annuals.

Kipling refers to India's naughty gangs of marauding monkeys as the *Bandar-log*. They are vastly entertaining to watch, with their acrobatic antics, often with a youngster slung on their back – but less funny when you realise that they have successfully raided your hotel room when you left the window open. You feel lucky if all they took were the bananas from the fruit bowl.

I was feeling slightly overwrought when I walked back to our bus through these gardens, where the naughty *Bandar-log* were carelessly grazing on the heads of the marigolds that were planted all along the gravel paths. Back on the bus Sally dashingly urged the coachman to drive us down to the Cauvery river, through fields of rice and corn which on her last visit had all been part of the Sultan's gardens, and I was almost overcome by my first real contact with India, which occurred when we arrived at the bank of the river, at the spot where the north and south branches of the river reunite below the island of Seringapatam.

Now the place where two rivers meet is considered auspicious in India, and this spot was one of those places I'd read of known as the Sacred Ghats, a concept I had found elusive and mysterious. What was the connection between the Western Ghats (mountains), ghats for ritual bathing and the burning ghats (funeral pyres)? The answer was revealed: here, the ghats were the rough uneven stone slabs leading down into the river for ritual bathing – simply, ghats means steps, of any scale. And all over these steps there were hundreds of people preparing for and in the midst of their devotions, braiding and unbraiding each other's ropes of long black hair, oiling and anointing and sprinkling ashes, chanting and meditating; flower petals lay all around as children splashed, old ladies wallowed and groups of young men laughed together. It was the most life-filled scene I have ever witnessed,

utterly unselfconscious and full of attentive love and social pleasure, alive with the mystery of faith, which most of us usually find so embarrassing and unwieldy – certainly in England. I longed to run away from my everyday life, so calm and pale-coloured by comparison, and never to leave; as I looked on I yearned for immersion, to be wrapped in jasmine garlands, showered with marigold petals (maybe I could substitute zinnia petals for an even more multi-coloured effect), then doused in patchouli and bathed in conviction. Instead I stood and stared in fascination, then turned away, got back on the bus and on we went.

DAL

Before this trip to India I saw dal as just one of the delicious things piled on to the hot plates in the middle of the table in the Cromer Tandoori, on a winter night out, following a trip to the cinema. In India I grasped that this is as staple as rice itself, and that any meal including breakfast might happily consist of a plate of rice, temptingly dented with the back of the spoon to make a bowl for a ladleful of dal.

With two vegetarians in the family, I often make dal. But I love it so much now that it's often what Matt and I choose for an easy supper, whether vegetarians are present or not. The basics are simple and the variants endless, which is probably why I like it so much.

While a splash of oil (peanut, grapeseed, olive, or recently coconut oil) is heating in a pan, I grind a selection of spices using a pestle and mortar. I rootle about in the cupboard in search of cardamom pods, coriander seeds, mustard seeds, a couple of cloves maybe, or a little piece of cinnamon bark, a shake of turmeric, some cumin seeds – in no particular combination. I grind my selection together with sea salt and peppercorns, then whoosh them into the oil, stirring to keep them from catching and revelling in the glorious smell. Recently I have substituted a spoonful or two of superior rose harissa for these spices with delicious results. I set this aside and chop a couple of onions, or a few spring onions, or a clove or two of garlic, then add this, with maybe some chopped chilli, to the spices and cook slowly until they are soft. Then I add lentils, green, yellow or red, rinsed if the packet says so, then stirred hissing into the onions and spices. I like to coat the lentils in oil and spices before I add water (or stock) and turn the heat down low so the whole can simmer aromatically until the lentils are soft and tender.

Morning Glory

In the early years of the company I romped through my favourite flowers, turning them into patterns with all haste and joy – I was continuously excited by the freedom offered by the huge foam sponges I could cut, at some points even causing spongeware to burst its pottery confines when I realised that we could print on windows, furniture and even walls.

A little after the arrival of the Morning Glory pattern, Matt and I conceived a project for printing a huge mural on the walls of our Fulham Road shop. We used the same drawings: at triple scale, mixed with lots of other flowers, fruits and even vegetables from our growing pattern books for a sponge-printing extravaganza. The design was simple: we made a framework of huge sections of bamboo, as in a real kitchen garden, with flowerpots at their feet, and we dipped the sponges in watered-down emulsion colours, to re-imagine the decorations celebrating the time of the harvest which Matt and I had seen in one of the Palladian villas in the Veneto.

> In the *Jardins Botaniques* in Paris, Matthew and I saw wigwams of pea sticks covered with so many different varieties of Morning Glory. All shades of pink, violet, purple and blue they varied from big bold trumpets to fairy sized flowers whose leaves seemed to have been delicately snipped into tiny fish bones.

Morning Glory worked fairly well on the pottery, and I drew from life in Mum's greenhouse at Minety, with a strong intention to capture the twisting vines of the plants – tendrils twirling out in search of new supports, with beautiful trumpets of Heavenly Blue (the name of Mum's favourite variety) bursting in all directions amongst heart-shaped leaves. But I always felt some frustration about having to contain and curb within the surface of a teapot or mug a plant whose nature is almost as vigorous, unruly and outward-bound as its wild cousin the unstoppable bindweed. While making the mural in Fulham, Deonne, our design assistant at the time, worked with me, and we egged each other on, with Matthew adding flourishes, so that I like to believe we succeeded in making something flamboyant and lush enough to utterly vanquish this slight feeling that I had not yet served the plant quite fairly.

We have often used large-scale sponges and emulsion paint to decorate panels and walls, sometimes for exhibition stands, and currently in the café in the factory, where Matthew had a set of Brown Kitchen sponges (see

page 208) made to embellish some of the walls when he furbished up these rooms which hadn't previously seen the light of day.

I should really try to describe Mum's greenhouse at Minety, as it was so very characteristic of her and her methods. When they bought the house in Minety, she and my stepfather Rick did a very gentle job on a fairly eccentric house, making it delightful, and just as much of a magnet as their first home at Rawlinson Road had ever been. They gained a bigger garden and three fields, swapping urban for country life with an emphasis on stables, and a longer trip to the station. My little sisters Nell and Clover were lent some fairly well-behaved ponies, who sometimes came into the kitchen for tea; Mum's aunt mustered a troop of bantams for her and they too paid kitchen visits; two kittens arrived from the vet in a cardboard box, and when some old friends retired from farming their middle-aged collie took up her position as guardian of the yard – causing some consternation amongst the postmen. The garden situation was made exciting by the fact that with the house came two men who both regarded the garden as their exclusive territory, an entrenched position made more complicated by the fact that they had apparently not been known to speak to each other for at least twelve years. Mum floated easily in just this sort of situation. I never heard her anything but affectionate and amused by both gardeners, but within a year or so, the more curmudgeonly of the two decided to retire, leaving the field to Mum and Bob. It may be that the greenhouse had been a focus in the great gardeners' feud, as work seems (in my memory) to have started on the greenhouse after the curmudgeon was gone.

Rick worked all week in London and he would throw himself energetically into gardening projects when he came home for the weekends. Meanwhile, Mum and Bob communed on weekdays, planning borders and schemes. There were always lots of capital projects, such as the pond which leaked, so was usually empty; the mysterious remnants of a moat, deep and murky and in need of clearing; the hedges, which badly wanted cutting and laying to stop the sheep from escaping; the clearing of a wilderness known as the Dell. There were conferences on these subjects, always open to all comers – but the most heartfelt of all of these was the greenhouse. This was to all intents and purposes derelict, its timber soft and flaky, paint all gone, and almost all the glass smashed; but Mum knew it as pivotal to her plans, and cajoled Rick into an everlasting round of running repairs. I don't think its glass was ever complete, and a crunchy underfoot texture was a constant feature; the opening and closing of its windows was a delicate operation, and yet throughout the summer Mum was always coaxing anyone who visited to 'Come and look at the greenhouse, do!' Because inside it she made her version of that ever-enticing busy and humid world. There were of course abundant tomatoes, and under Bob's influence these were high-yielding – but this was before today's obsessive interest (positive, but confusing!) in obscure varieties – of which I know Bob would have taken a dim view. Beneath the tomatoes she planted basil, again in generous quantities; and through all of this twisted the tendrils of her favourite thing of all, which was the morning glory. She especially loved to remind people like me, who would arrive in the greenhouse at eleven or twelve yawning and carrying a cup of coffee: 'Oh. Such a pity you didn't get here earlier, the morning glories are almost over now, but earlier they were perfection. Now do pick some basil for Matthew to make some pesto, and we really must get on with lunch.'

MACARONI CHEESE WITH BOILED POTATOES AND A GARLICKY GREEN SALAD AFTER

Because this was what we had for lunch on Saturdays often and often. So it reminds me of Minety, where Mum's kitchen was a dark room on the northern side of the house, so always a blessed relief in summer, but warmed by the Aga to be cosy in cold weather as well.

This was one of Mum's favourite lunches: she first ate it as cooked by her wonderful, much-adored Aunt Letty, who was a huge inspiration to her.

Always use spaghetti (*not* macaroni), the brand which comes in a blue paper packet for nostalgic pleasure, and quarter two large onions into the salted boiling water before adding the pasta.

Make your cheese sauce with lots of strong Cheddar, plenty of French mustard and a good half of a nutmeg, grated. The sauce must be plentiful and runny so that the final result is juicy rather than solid!

When the al dente pasta is stirred into the cheese sauce and poured into a shallow earthenware dish, sprinkle the top with sliced tomatoes, grated Parmesan, and a handful of breadcrumbs before baking in a hot oven.

And as Aunt Letty always said, there are few things more delicious than almost-burned cheese sauce, bubbling and browning around the edge of the baking dish – so be sure not to take this out of the oven too soon.

Red Flower

My younger sisters have, unsurprisingly, numerous friends – a rainbow host; they were children, then teenagers growing up, while I was grappling toddlers, changing nappies and generally rather hard at work on the coalface of family life, and this colourful host has always been fascinating to me. I feel especially happy to have a great big tribe of siblings (there are eight of us, the produce of three separate marriages) and also to be the oldest of them all. I love my vantage point, I hugely enjoy the perspective, and now that my children are growing up I can see the crowd of my younger siblings' friends more clearly. Some have babies of their own, some are married, some are buckling down while others are resisting, still floating free. At a party recently I watched one of these latter group; tall and willowy, she is beautiful in a delicious, negligent sort of way and she floated from garden to garden and in and out of the kitchen, like the elusive girl in the song, moving through the fair. She was wearing a long flounced cotton dress, a Laura Ashley print and thus a survivor from the seventies; close up it had a few battle scars, but it suited her style so perfectly. As I drove home I tried to work out the precise way in which Laura Ashley's style worked; why did that unsophisticated dress suit such a glamorous girl so beautifully, so many years later? How does a simple, simple print pack such a punch?

All designing is a process of distillation. We are in constant pursuit of the perfect marriage of form, function and decoration, plucking themes, ideas, attitudes and moods from all over as we think our way towards the cleanest expression, the truest, the most personal and honest way to evolve a true signature. And this process continues in a broader sense throughout all of our lives; whether cautiously or exuberantly, we are all making our mark, consciously and unconsciously we sift the options – as we choose a dress, shop for food, cook a meal for friends and while we furnish our homes – it's all designing; and we always write in our very own style.

Laura Ashley was a natural and confident designer, whose handwriting is still clear, legible and authoritative. She offered us all a wonderfully easy and compelling new vocabulary and as soon as her dresses existed you could not imagine a summer morning without them in the world, because they presented us with the means to describe ourselves as beautiful in a sweetly disordered way. But the dress itself was not sexy – in fact Laura Ashley was a byword for well-behaved. It was all up to you. When you put one of those dresses on you could be whichever heroine you chose to be.

One of her dresses made a whole finished outfit (bare feet a given, hair long and rippling); the shapes aligned us with Thomas Hardy's heroines, always just a little bit Bathsheba, the flounces added Laurie Lee's whirling, giggling sisters to the picture, the surprising new colours added impact, and the prints – oh, the prints! Although Laura Ashley prints may well have been drawn closely from original Victorian wallpapers and cottons, they were appropriated entirely for the brand, wholly owned, completely assimilated into one signature.

For the most part they were stylised florals, with endless variations on a flowery, leafy sprig, and this was all I had in mind when I drew and cut the sponges for the pattern called Red Flower. I wanted to make a recessive pattern, one which stood back modestly, apparently demure like Laura Ashley's girls. But offering to adapt itself to your style. Variations on flowers and leaves are everywhere in decoration, but in this specific case I am talking about flowers and leaves which have been stylised to the point of decorative anonymity. Usually I love to find an economical but telling way to describe a very particular plant (or animal, or whatever), but it is liberating to push beyond the descriptive towards the purely decorative. And this is the field of ancient peasant craft – of simple earthenware plates daubed with fat, friendly flowers; of coarse linen tablecloths and runners embroidered with running, twining clusters of pretty and unidentifiable flowers; of decorative panels on heavy carved wooden furniture – the very essence of family and village life all over Europe until television slayed unselfconscious craft, pretty much in a generation.

LIZ'S CHEESECAKE

A seventies classic to eat while wearing vintage farmgirl style.

Serves 8

1 x 250g packet of 'Nice' biscuits | 100g butter, melted
225g full fat cream cheese (such as Philadelphia) | 50g caster sugar
3 large free-range egg yolks | Finely grated zest of 2 unwaxed lemons
300ml single cream | 200g fresh raspberries | 25g icing sugar

Preheat the oven to 150°C/130°C Fan/Gas 2. Crush the 'Nice' biscuits into fine crumbs and mix with the melted butter. Press them on to the base of a shallow, 20cm, round loose-bottomed cake tin and leave to set in the fridge for at least 20 minutes.

Cream together the cream cheese, caster sugar, egg yolks, half the lemon zest and the single cream until smooth. Pour the mixture on to the biscuit base and bake on the middle shelf of the oven for 40–50 minutes, until just set but still slightly wobbly. Leave to cool, then chill in the fridge for at least 2 hours.

To serve, carefully remove the cheesecake from the tin and transfer it to a flat serving plate. Crush the raspberries with the icing sugar to make a purée and rub through a sieve into a bowl, discarding the seeds left behind. Serve the cheesecake with the raspberry sauce poured over and sprinkled with the rest of the lemon zest.

ANIMALS

I can only think of a couple of patterns produced by Emma Bridgewater over the years which feature exotic, foreign *zoo* animals, and they are Animals Parade and a mug called Blue Zoo. These are literally the only ones I can think of, and they are both drawn by Matt. There is a reason for this, which is simple: I didn't like the zoo when I was little. I felt daunted, slightly over-awed and never entirely happy there. It was a splendid sight to see the elephants being hosed and scrubbed with yard brushes by their keepers but their poos were *enormous*. I'm sure I shrieked with laughter with all the other children to see the chimps dressed up in children's clothes to have a tea party. But afterwards it gave me what my daughter Margaret calls Bad Thoughts, by which she means nightmares, of having to join in with them. I would infinitely rather play with a model farm than a zoo, and I didn't think I ever wanted to go to Africa to see the wild animals in the bush. Actually this turned out to be hokum, because I could not have been more excited than I was to be taken to the Kabini game reserve in India in 2014, where I was enchanted by it all. I saw elephants, a tiger, countless monkeys, amazing birds and enjoyed myself almost immoderately.

Which says that I have perhaps grown out of what was only ever a mild aversion, but there it is. Underneath I'd always turn first to homely species. I think I feel more at home with mice and rabbits, with or without little jackets and muslin dresses on, than with big fierce beasts. Give me a lurcher over a wolf, a robin rather than a drongo – whether racquet-tailed or not. And any chicken trumps any exotic parrot.

Hunting

Old spongeware is often funny, sometimes on purpose. As a genre it has a naïveté which was really what first drew me to it. It is as if it was decorated while the paintress was thinking about something else, as the motifs are often incongruous.

In my mind it is as if, as designs multiplied, lots of sponges were cut, and gradually they accumulated in a big box, and each decorator rootled through, chose her personal favourite motifs from this big random collection, then selected colours and set about decorating the ware as it came to hand, to please herself rather than to obey a set of instructions. The ware itself doesn't speak of matching dinner services, and it is sometimes damaged under the glaze, by which I mean even before it was decorated, so it might have been bought very cheaply, and possibly on as random a basis as the choice of sponges. All these impressions are pleasing to me, as they play directly towards the iconic image, always in my mind's eye, of Mum's dresser. The arrangement of her crockery was apparently a happy accident, but in fact it was underpinned with principles of personal selection on a low budget, leaving her to focus on the food and the company, in the most relaxed and enjoyable atmosphere, with just the right kit to hand to augment the warmth and welcome of every meal there.

The patterns often contain animals, but they seem to feature incidentally rather than as the stars of the pottery.

At first I imitated this laid-back attitude and went in for some fairly kooky mixtures. But within a few months I was starting to feel that the technique belonged to me and that I could use it to convey my own personal ideas. And one of my very first coherent original designs was Hunting, closely followed by Farmyard.

I really enjoyed fiddling with the drawings of the animals, pushing for a result which retained complete simplicity, in keeping with the genre, and at the same time conveying in a few lines the characteristic of the animal I wanted. So I set out to make a rabbit running at full pelt (but still somehow obviously near enough to the hole to escape.) Next, running in the opposite direction, to gently laugh at the brainlessness of their kind, I made an elegant greyhound, running much more for pleasure than blood lust. Lastly I drew a duck, startled by all this dashing about, as if rising out of a tussocky place in the field – signified only by green bands – where this hunting scene takes place. I taught myself to do banding in the course of my early decorating experiments, never very skilfully, but so that I could incorporate bands wherever I wanted to while designing.

I felt instantly sure that both Hunting and Farmyard would go into a saleable collection, and indeed they were featured on the second leaflet I made to send out to prospective customers. Of the pair, Farmyard fared better and stayed in

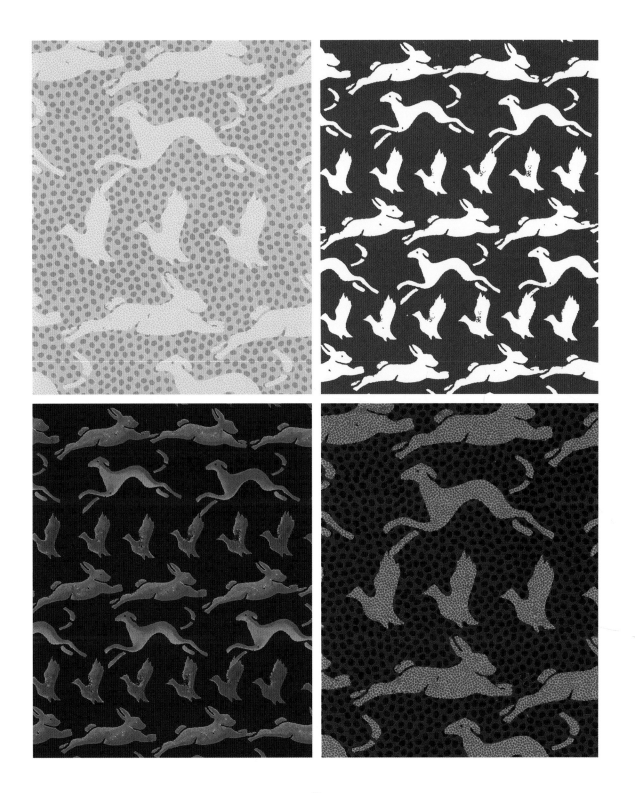

the collection for some time; moreover, we have re-introduced it a couple of times. But I am particularly fond of Hunting. This is probably because as a family we have always loved lurchers, and I have also flirted with Italian greyhounds, and we currently have an especially beautiful, utterly brainless whippet.

Eastwood Works was one of a cluster of big factories in Hanley standing amidst terraces of houses, schools, shops and pubs. Now an empty field stretches out behind it. We hope the factory will be at the heart of the community that will live here in the future.

We constantly revisit our archive, and scrutinise an old design for new possibilities. This is not just thrift, and a recycling habit now so deeply ingrained in the collective psyche, but rather it springs from my conviction that while I will not get hung up on the old Potteries promise to stock a pattern for ever and a day (totally impractical for a factory), I really love to create echoes and re-echoes in the collections over the years, so that as people build their collections they will find familiar themes, colour schemes and motifs recurring.

This is one of my earliest patterns, and quite old-fashioned. It owes something to the charming Wedgwood Hunting pattern, itself my favourite amongst the numerous long-gone patterns based on sentimental depictions of old England; favourite themes, on quantities of wares, now mostly gathering dust in charity shops, include Coaching Inns, Village Greens, and many variations on Hunting scenes. Our factory in Hanley was one of three built by the Meakin family in 1882, and was always known as Eastwood Works. By 1887, through family mergers and skilful planning, J. & G. Meakin was recognised as one of the biggest potteries in the country. The family focused on export, their markets being the USA, Canada, Australia and New Zealand, and I imagine that these markets may have been especially susceptible to such gently nostalgic themes. But they were an adventurous and adaptable company, even if their wares were not always in the very best possible taste. By 1950 Meakin were making a million pieces of ware a week, but their fortunes changed in the 60s, and they were taken over by Johnsons.

My father-in-law, Peter Rice, loves to buy me coffee pots from the 60s and 70s. Which were, as it turned out, the dying days of the brand J. & G. Meakin. I feel huge affection for their 'Art' ranges, perhaps slightly because they make Pat (my mother-in-law), squeal with horror, but mostly for sheer sentimentality. If I say some of their names, you will get the picture: Celeste, Aztec, Sunflower ... And Pat was right, those designs were not good enough to keep the company afloat. Neither art nor nostalgia could keep the factory going, and Johnsons' massive-selling tableware pattern Eternal Beau was not enough to keep that factory alive: Johnsons went down, finally, in 2004, swallowed up by Wedgwood. Eastwood had already been standing empty for some time when we bought it in 1996.

An old-fashioned pattern such as Hunting calls for a traditional favourite lunch. For a delicious cottage pie, whether made with top-quality minced steak, cheap mince of dubious DNA, or the finely chopped remains of the Sunday roast beef, all you need to add is frozen peas and tomato ketchup. We often serve this at our Factory Lunches, with a delicious claret to thank our guests for making the trip to Hanley, and I especially like that you only need a fork to eat it, and there need be no distractions to spoil the flow of conversation.

Blue Hens

We had, as I have said, a very mixed collection of pottery in the kitchen in my childhood. Mum bought almost no contemporary tableware, preferring to build up her collection in junk shops and markets. I can remember two exceptions to this, the first a simple set of white pottery plates, cups and saucers with wide pink bands on the rims. She liked these because they looked like the china used in the burrow of Old Mrs Rabbit – the Flopsy Bunnies drink their camomile tea from exactly these cups. Matthew says that his mum bought the pale blue version at the same time. Both came from Habitat, as did the only other commercially available dinnerware to catch Mum's fancy, although it was a long way from being a contemporary pattern: this was Brown Quails, a veteran pattern from Furnivals. It was probably a recent casualty of these on the kitchen floor that had prompted my fruitless search for cups and saucers for her birthday, invoking the Damascene moment when I knew that I was to make kitchen pottery. Simply replacing Brown Quails seemed a bit dull, an uninspired sort of gift. The design was also available in blue; lovely, but still not enough of a departure.

I didn't produce a design on a poultry theme at the very beginning, but I did turn to chickens pretty quickly, adding Black Cockerel to the collection in 1987. You might remember some other Emma Bridgewater poultry patterns, for example Starry Hens (2004), or the fine rooster by Mark Hearld in the Blue Animals group from 2005, or earlier, from 1999, some lovely blue baby mugs featuring a pigeon, a goose and a guinea fowl. Now poultry is an honourable decorative theme, resort of tableware designers of all stripes, my most favourite of which must be the totally wonderful Luneville chickens design, in an especially pretty shade of pink, called Chanteclerc. I also relish the flocks of turkeys and quails featured on two dominant and beautiful patterns from Spode, often aimed at an export market, namely Woodland and Byron. Much of the ware produced in these designs was doubtless destined for the USA (for Thanksgiving dinner tables, I assume). But in a way I love them all, including the humble chickens on Sadler's everyday ware, and the chickens in a snowstorm produced in the 80s at Burgess & Leigh – Chanticleer.

We produced our Blue Hens design ten years later, in 1997, and at first it was only available on a mug; but the choice of classic cobalt blue was fortuitous, as the result is that our Blue Hens, which we eventually realised (doh!) would do well as a whole set of shapes, could be, and often is, mixed freely with the huge number of other pottery patterns available in this truly perfect colour. The Potteries produced millions of acres of dinner wares decorated with blue transfer patterns; the designs were numerous, but they very frequently harped on the theme of landscapes, often typically English ones, featuring lots of rural, sentimental, domestic, familiar scenes, many farmyard related.

Before I return to actual chickens, I *think* it's fair to include the pheasant in this poultry theme, because there are flocks of pheasants on china – I'm not sure that pheasants actually come in flocks, I will have to ask a gamekeeper and report back to you – and I want to include the marvellous and incredibly long-lived pale blue transferware pattern called Asiatic Pheasant by Burgess & Leigh in this scenic blue pottery muster, in order to throw a brief gleam on the commercial tenacity of the Potteries in their heyday. When a pattern 'took' on the market, as this did in the 1830s, every single manufacturer, so it seems, would leap on to the bandwagon and produce a variant on whatever the new fashion might be. Taking just this one theme, if I list just a few of the ancestors and contemporaries of this design you will see what I mean: Myott's Chelsea Bird; Royal Stafford's Asiatic Pheasant; Churchill's Wildlife; Crown Ducal's Bristol Asiatic Pheasant; Davenport no. 6 Asiatic Pheasant; John Meir's Asiatic Pheasant; Enoch Wedgwood's Asiatic Pheasant; Johnsons' Asiatic you know what …

> I assumed that the sole purpose of a pottery hen on her nest was to hold Smarties, as our white Portmeirion one from my childhood was filled with them. Apparently not: the base is for hot water to keep the breakfast boiled eggs warm.

The list is long, though I have not been exhaustive. The different makers are often impossible to ascertain, due to erratic back-stamping and the tangled business alliances of Stoke-on-Trent, where takeovers, mergers and bust-ups make provenance hard to determine in the case of Asiatic Pheasants, and indeed many other patterns.

I want to be clear about this: while I deplore actual shameless copying, I have to remind myself that there is after all nothing new under the sun. We are all recycling ideas already treated by many before us: the challenge is to make a theme your very own, by passing that old idea through a brand new filter. So I love it when I find an original twist on the pheasant theme, for example A. J. Wilkinson's beautiful Chintz, a black transferware pattern featuring pheasants which are beautifully hand-coloured. Or Myott's Old Bow Pheasant. Moreover, I know that I find it sensible, pleasing even, to imagine the collective wringing-out of all the goodness, or commercial viability, from a theme by a market, as I like thoroughness, and I feel intuitively that this was the spirit that

built the Potteries. It feels vigorous, determined, good. And finally, as Burgess & Leigh, whose own Pheasant variant was by no means the first on the block, show us – the battle will finally go to the one who simply keeps struggling on.

While visiting Pompeii, and later, with the children, Herculaneum, followed by the marvellous Archaeological Museum in Naples to see the actual stuff from the ruins – the frescoes, the mosaics, the oil lamps and the ceramics – I was struck by the familiarity of many of the themes chosen for decoration by the ancient Romans. I could actually only find a chicken featured as dinner, for the cat, on a game-dealer's shop sign, or, best of all, as a lone foot amongst the litter following a feast on a *trompe-l'œil* floor. Actually this last is from Heraklitos, but throughout you don't have to look hard to spot that there is a sweet feeling of pleasure in domestic animals, from dogs and cats to sheep, goats, peacocks, pigeons and quails. And when I find an actual live chicken on, say, a piece of Arretine pottery, I will report. Meanwhile I can readily instance the use of dramatically plumaged roosters (OK, some of them *might* be pheasants) on Qing cups, Ming vases, and any number of Famille Rose wares, because for the Chinese, the pheasant is a symbol of luck and happiness, which is a happy thought. All in all, I feel confident to assert the extreme constancy of the appeal of poultry on pottery.

Mum always had a troupe of bantams, and at Bassingbourn she had white fantail pigeons too, who arranged themselves most beautifully on the barn roof. But poultry really only arrived fully fledged, so to speak, in my life when I met Matthew in 1987. He is something of a specialist in the matter of keeping small caged animals, including, especially, chickens. He grew up on Chiswick Mall with parents who had met at the Royal College of Art and whose whole lives until Matt's birth had been dedicated to design; Pat has an auxiliary qualification in shopping, particularly for handbags, at which she excels, while Peter would I think prefer to spend any time over from designing for the theatre and opera on life-drawing classes or silent films. So it must have been a shock when Matthew early on showed his true colours: he wanted to raise animals, and not just a couple of hamsters. From an early age he kept small birds – canaries and quails, to be followed by rabbits. He took to chickens after he went to Bedales, keeping a flock in his parents' back garden and a second illicit flock hidden in the garden of an empty house near the school. Eventually he acquired ducks, guinea fowl and geese: the whole story was what he was after. And he wanted to cook and eat these pets, not just draw them.

Pat and Peter rented a cottage on an estate in Sussex, conveniently close to the theatre in Chichester where Peter was working at the time, and once there Matthew's interest immediately widened to include all farming, forestry,

gardening – but particularly as it affected the kitchen, and also shooting. When we got married, we bought a house by the traffic lights opposite the library on the western reaches of the Fulham Road. The garden was soon full of poultry, and the vision of Matthew flitting along the back garden walls, waving a landing net, in pursuit of escapees became familiar locally. The neighbours were very tolerant about this. Next door lived a kind croupier who was happy to feed the fowl when we were away, in exchange for their eggs. In Norfolk the flock reached epic proportions, with at one stage a large pre-Christmas flock of friendly, always slightly shocked-looking turkeys; we also kept quails for their eggs, guinea fowl to make the garden more exotic and peacocks for their great beauty. So we have never been short of models for this theme.

Labradors

When you get bad news – your exam grades are too low for the university you set your heart on, your girlfriend changes her status to single on Facebook, when you burn the brownies or drop your phone down the loo, with all your contacts on it – who do you turn to? Your darling cosy Labrador of course. You could lower yourself and tell the cat, but she would be so obviously disdainful. And she probably knew about it before you anyway, being a bit psychic and not in a nice way. Or you could hug the whippet and whisper in her ear – she would be sympathetic, but she wouldn't understand a word you said. The great thing, the best thing about Labs is that they really, really care about your feelings. And they understand what you tell them. Well, that's my explanation, totally scientific, obviously, as to why we are all so devoted to these typically English family pets.

What are the things that feel like home? There are hundreds of things, but I would instantly cite the smell of a log fire in the house, a huge bunch of roses in the hall, macaroni cheese for lunch on Saturday and a sofa on which the whole family can pile up to watch *Some Like It Hot* on a wet afternoon. We would all need to add our personal markers – the theme tune to *The Archers*, the cosy Aga, stephanotis bath oil; a colander of the first broad beans, or the sound of a clutch under pressure as the parents arrive for lunch. But I think that very few people would want to leave the Labrador, stretched out on that sofa all over his or her family, off that list.

In Martha's Vineyard, in a venerable old smugglers' shack on the quay, in a shop called The Black Dog, they have raised the black Lab to its rightful position as cult object. Or so my mother-in-law believes; she can't resist any type of merchandise from their shop, because everything, and I mean everything, in the shop is printed with a black Lab, even things that she doesn't like, such as baseball caps and T-shirts. When we went to this shop, in September, a perfect time, when most of the island was blissfully peaceful, and the beaches were deserted while the sea was still delicious for swimming, we found a feeding frenzy of shoppers. And we joined in helplessly, piling pyjamas and hoodies at the cash desk, because we could think of so many people who would be as charmed as we were. It's quite a thought, a whole buzzing retail business – plus an ice cream stand, and a restaurant serving a top breakfast menu with a delightful harbour to gaze across while we waited for our coffee, hash browns and bacon – all centred on a black dog bearing a close resemblance to a Labrador. Because in fact, on closer inspection it's clear that this is that other favourite, a Lab-type, with in this case a touch of mastiff in its parentage. But let's not quibble.

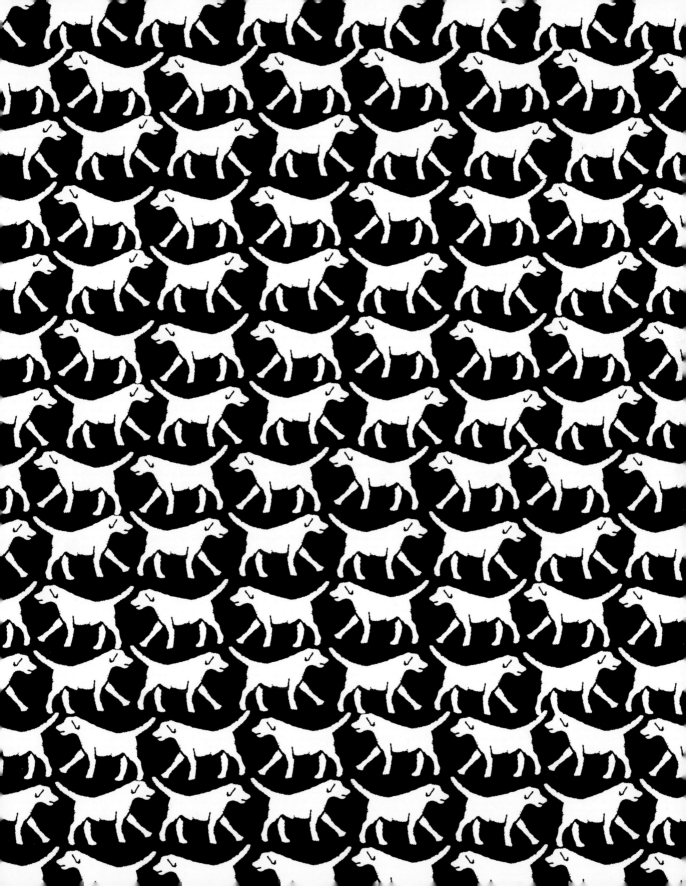

My father had Labradors, usually pale yellow ones, and he only recently converted to the even more communicative company of lurchers. (Not on any account to be confused with whippets, these elegant crossbreeds can be the most companionable of dogs, even, to my way of thinking, better company in bed, car and on sofa than a Labrador.) Pop's yellow Labs, Molly, then Lily, were more beach companions, keepers of the sandcastle and watchers over the piles of surfers' towels, than gun-dogs. But Matthew has been faithful to brand Labrador all his life, and as just one of their many roles in his life, all of his dogs have been good (if sometimes very enthusiastic) gun-dogs. His parents forbade him to play with guns as a child. I don't know if this had any direct effect, but when I met him he was more devoted to shooting than anyone I had ever met. And I got over my surprise more easily when I realised that he was equally, and slightly unusually among sportsmen, devoted to plucking, cooking and eating the trophies he brought home at the end of each day. Hare shooting upsets me; much pheasant shooting is dull and excessive; a barrage of lead seems a cruel welcome for storm-tossed woodcock and I quickly found that I was not prepared to take part in the decoying of ducks. Yet over the years I have also learned that a farm managed for the benefit of English partridges is also very attractive to me; I am thrilled by the occasions when I have got up before dawn to try to sneak out to a distant marsh where the wild geese just might fly over at sunrise, and most importantly, I know that a shooting lunch can be one of the most congenial of social events.

Matthew says that his vision of the civility of a shooting lunch was born when his friend Max described to him a day in the 1970s when he and his wife drove down into the Maremma from Florence, invited to a shooting lunch in an uninhabited *casa colonica*, where a long table snaked through the empty rooms, the company was glamorous and mixed, including many, like themselves, invited for the feast rather than the shooting, and the food was sublime. (I asked Max about this recently, and he said that I had completely garbled all the details, but *yes!* It had been lovely.) We may not have reached this peak of rustic but still Fellini-flavoured Dolce Vita yet, but Matthew always organises a very delicious event. We have introduced to these lunches friends, neighbours, all the beaters and whoever is attending meetings in the studio on the day. When we built a veranda on to our house in Norfolk, I was inattentive while Matt paced it out and murmured that we should be able to seat at least forty out there, but I soon learned what he had in mind. In fact, we are very committed to seating everyone at the same table, or as few tables as possible, for all types of feasting. There is something utterly, fundamentally good about sitting together around a long table, enticingly laid out for a big meal.

And if, as we do, you concentrate your shooting early in the season, all done by Christmas, then these feasts can combine shooting with Harvest Festival.

We are usually around thirty for his shooting lunches, and they are noisy, friendly events, with a marvellous bonus – they are over within an hour, to enable a last drive or two in the waning afternoon. Or another session in the studio. This is a very satisfactory form of entertaining.

At a shooting lunch Matt might serve up big steaming bowls containing beef stew, slowly cooked borlotti beans and baked potatoes. At Wickmere we would have apple and quince crumble and custard to follow, because there was a huge fruit supply. We have a few years before this is possible in Bampton, but the trees have been planted.

Dancing Mice

It's always an interesting challenge to make a pattern for children that really works. I am ever aware that we are up against themes with huge marketing muscle behind them. Children are shamelessly and ruthlessly sold to, and while I am constantly surprised and impressed by the sophistication with which they dodge through this thicket, nevertheless it's very tough to make a new voice heard in this market without a cartoon franchise and a breakfast cereal packet offer, a burger chain tie-in with a free plastic figurine and a TV advertising campaign. You doubt me? Just think about the paraphernalia associated with any of the following children's characters: Barbie! Thomas the Tank Engine. Spongebob Squarepants. Ice Age, Peppa Pig and Postman Pat. They all come with a vast franchise, which usually generates something approximating to a set of china along the way, and relentless publicity arrangements; in short, they dominate. Even Peter Rabbit. But he is one of my literary heroes, and it's been a privilege to put him, and Flopsy, on Emma Bridgewater mugs. Unfortunately, thanks to his savvy management, he is less than lucrative for us, as we have to pay a licence fee to use Beatrix Potter's illustrations. Matthew with his business hat on says don't let's – but as I say, it's a privilege and we had to do it.

But how are we to create our own characters? Royal Doulton did this very authoritatively when they launched Bunnikins in 1936. And it seems to me that much of the continued long-standing success of this (very enviably commercial) design by Sister Mary Barbara Vernon is due to the simple fact that the company stuck with it. After nearly eighty years Bunnikins is still a player, and it is still on the market today.

Over the years we have done several different children's things: diminutive pottery tea-sets, melamine mugs and plates, cutlery, and several different ideas for decorative themes. To begin with we stuck firmly to the old-fashioned monochrome look of Victorian Sunday School presents for all our children's designs, as in A Present for a Good Girl, and nursery rhymes such as Pussy Cat, Pussy Cat, and When Little Hen, hoping that if we kept it classic we could find a niche.

Niche it was and niche it remained. These black transfers, made in the old-fashioned way from actual copper plates, which turned out to be some of the very last ones engraved in Stoke, may have been economical (just one colour) to print, but they lacked easy appeal. The breakthrough came when we started to have a real success with our Birds designs in 2002; baby birds were an obvious next step, so we did Chicks, then Ducklings on baby mugs, baby bowls and little plates, and sales perked up.

Then we kind of lost touch with this area, directly related to the fact that my older daughters Lil and Kitty were growing up; we tuned in again a little later by conducting a ramshackle campaign of market research to find out what children really like. What we learnt was that they are picky, discerning, critical, and in the case of our own children easily bored by the whole pottery topic, especially when it threatened to make tea take too long; in fact a hard market to crack. If you get it wrong they swerve round it – Matt's Pink Fairy design (yes, this was slightly despairing, he was roundly bored by Barbie and she was much around in our family thanks to his mother's passion for her, but I bullied him to do a design to this brief) was treated with disdain by Margy and her friends – 'Dad, she is a bit fat, and not really pretty at all.' So it is as I started out by saying, a challenge.

Dancing Mice has been a success for us because we really did tap into a true enthusiasm, one shared by lots of children, by which I mean pet mice. I am perfectly certain that children have been taming mice and carrying them about in their pockets since the Stone Age. Michael was no exception – he kept pet mice for several years and they gave us all lots of fun. Actually not absolutely everyone. Phil is our friend and a top-class builder; he is tough and practical but appalled by mice: he really hates them. Michael's mice lived in a rather superior home, a large aquarium donated by friends when all their tropical fish were dead, and then they tired of watching the (vicious!) antics of crayfish retrieved from the stream in their garden. The mouse-arium lived on a table in an outdoors passage beside our office, and it often had to be shunted out of the way for projects. If Phil was involved he could barely stand to see them scuttle, and he especially despised the notion of actually buying food for them. Can't you just give them a carpet tile? was his bitter reaction. They lived in sawdust, and through their glass walls you could see into their nests: totally fun. If not as far as Phil was concerned.

But I'm jumping ahead; I want to tell you about their acquisition – they did not come from a pet shop. Mikey's birthday is between Christmas and the New Year, a far from ideal arrangement about which I always feel bad, as it falls inevitably at a time when the party spirit is at a low ebb, and present-giving can lack inspiration. It was exactly like this for his fifth birthday; I can't remember what I gave him, but I'm sure he would have had a pile of parcels to unwrap at breakfast. However, his main present, the one he really wanted, was not there, and instead, propped up on the parcels, was a beautifully decorated envelope containing ... a Mouse Token. No sign of the actual creatures which Mikey had been asking for very consistently.

MICE AT P

Now I had tried, I assure you – I'd been at it in a distracted way since well before Christmas and I'd been to several local pet shops. But there was a policy operating in all the places I visited, which I found baffling and jolly annoying, which is that you had to – get this – *apply* to buy a mouse. You had to put your name down, then come back in two weeks' time and sign a paper saying that you really had considered the implications of keeping creatures in cages, etc., etc. I hadn't done this. Partly because it made me so cross, but mostly in hopes of finding a less bossy shop. Anyway, some days passed after his birthday, and what with having lots going on we still had not fixed up the redemption of the Mouse Token. Michael was good-natured, but his sisters were increasingly militant on his behalf.

Then, as the new year of 2006 got under way, it was time to hold our Emma Bridgewater January sale, of which we had an outpost in the village hall on the green in Aldborough. For the first day it was all hands on deck, as we were furiously busy. At teatime on the second day it calmed down, and I knew that the shops would be back to normal, so Mikey, Margy and I, along with a friend of Kitty's called Ivan, drove to North Walsham. This is the kind of town where I very much hoped I might be able to overcome the whole mouse-is-for-life-not-for-Christmas malarkey, if indeed I encountered it there. As we left, Matthew came after us with a teapot containing more than £7,000, as we always tried not to have too much cash with us in the village hall. I wrapped it in a coat in the boot and off we went. The pet shop in the Market Place had no mice. Crisis. Michael was very sad. I looked around frantically for inspiration, while Margy and Ivan tried to persuade him that a hamster, or a guinea pig, would be just as much fun, but no dice. There were two girls of about ten mooching about looking at pet accessories, experts basically, and I turned to them and asked where the best pet shop was, after this one. They said Norwich, but it was too late, they would soon be closing. Did they keep mice at home? I asked wildly. No. Hamsters. But their stepfather kept mice. Loads of them and they smelt a bit. Do you think he would sell me a pair? I asked. They were not sure, but not disconcerted, so I pressed on. Please could I ring him up? And ask him, now? Realising this sounded a bit eccentric to them, I tried a different tack: if I lent them my phone would they ring home and ask?

Well, they went into a huddle, while the pet shop lady eyed me up and down. Then they agreed to call their mum; I spoke to her, explained the situation, and, oh joy! She said she couldn't imagine why anyone would want the stinky things, but yeah, I could come round. The girls gave me directions, and set off ahead of us, arriving at the same moment. North Walsham was our shopping town when we first went to Norfolk, and I love it. Actually I loved it much more before Sainsbury's arrived and killed the market place, but that's life. It is a nice town, just a little bit rough around the edges, and the girls lived on an estate whose status was hard to assess, as it was now dark; there were a few car seats arranged haphazardly around a tree, and some cars which might not see a motorway again – however, this was not a time to hesitate. Thinking of the teapot in the boot, I told Ivan to lounge about against the car; he was to look tough, maybe roll a cigarette.

We held sales in the Village Hall on Aldborough Green for several years. The queues were legendary, and the customers amazingly patient as we struggled more or less accurately to tot up each bill without benefit of scanners, tills, or even calculators.

The girls let us in breathlessly and their mum was friendly and sent us out to the garden shed, where the girls' stepfather followed us. There was an enormous crate, heaving with mice; Michael was overjoyed and the kind chap started fishing them out for him to look at. He chose a sweet pair, boy and girl, one a chic beige, the other a more raffish pale skewbald, and these were put into a cardboard box for Michael, and he and Margy argued busily about names. Meanwhile a deal was struck, and although the nice man said he would only charge a pound each I gave him a fiver, as I was so fervently grateful. An uneasy thought had occurred to me. I'd suppressed it, but now that I was flushed with triumph and relief I dared to ask: why did he keep so many mice? For the snakes, of course. Yikes. My worst nightmare. We were very close to what must, from the look of their larder, be a large reptile collection. Would we like to see them? Me, I'd rather be boiled in oil, but of course Michael and even Margy were keen as mustard. The mice were kept in the shed (the smell), but the snakes, they needed the central heating, so of course they were in the living-room. I hovered miserably in the hall, feeling deep anxiety at the thought of what was on the other side of the wall, until the children came out and we said our goodbyes and went to join Ivan outside. He had had a quiet time, no excitements; no one had tried to hold him up and nick the polka dot teapot; the children wanted to go back, so that he too should see the snakes, but I was not hanging about, as it was time to go home and make supper.

This original pair bred prodigiously in their mouse-arium. Because of them Mikey acquired the nickname Mousey; he did a desultory mouse trade among his friends, and sometimes when he was at school I would liberate a few of them in the field to keep the population under control. They were engaging models, and Matthew drew them carefully and lovingly. We all liked them, and they often came to tea, played in Margaret's doll's house, had Lego vehicles built for them and all that sort of thing. So it was inevitable that they would feature in a children's pattern. On return from a holiday in Spain, with a trio of deeply wonderful lunette dresses for the dressing-up box, the idea of dressing the mice as if for a party evolved quite naturally. Which is always the best way.

HASTY TEATIMES

Ideas for when you have stayed out later than you meant to might include;

Pesto can be thrown together while the pasta boils, using, when the cupboard is a bit bare, any oil (rapeseed is actually quite good), any grated cheese – even Cheddar – any nuts, even ground almonds if that's all you have, and a chopped handful of any green herbs. Just pound them all together in a pestle and mortar.

Eggy bread is French toast when it's not in America: just beat a couple of eggs, then dip into them some thick slices of bread and fry the bread in butter until golden. Good just like that with salt and pepper or as a pudding version, sprinkled with icing sugar.

You can make **lightning pizzas** by improvising on slices of bread, spreading them with tomato purée, then grated cheese, herbs, maybe olives, anchovies, really whatever you can find that is popular. Before cooking, dribble a little olive oil over them – and best to heat these pizzas in the oven until sizzling; the grill is less satisfactory.

Bubble and squeak is a cinch, as long as you have some leftover veg in the larder – preferably mashed potato and cabbage or sprouts, though really any combo can be tarted up with some cheese grated on top of the veg mix while it fries slowly in the frying pan. My children like chilli sauce to squirt over, and don't forget the tomato ketchup ... You could add an egg, fried or poached, on top.

Corned beef hash is an acquired taste, which I definitely have, and it's a popular tea thing in our family, when made like this: fry a sliced onion or two gently in a little oil in a heavy pan. Meanwhile boil some potatoes and open a can of corned beef (quite an art, good luck); then, when the onions are soft, bash up the potatoes a bit, break up the beef with a fork and roughly mix both with the onions in the frying pan. Fry gently until a delicious browned crust forms (don't fiddle with it!), and serve with tomato ketchup, chilli sauce, chutney, etc.

Bird & Worm

I had done lots of freeform designs, departing from the more traditional repeating look of old spongeware, when I sat down to draw the motifs for this pattern, but I am always drawn back to the simplicity of simple repeats, and it doesn't get much more basic than this. But I think it works. And I think that is always down to rhythm: you need a pleasing sense of movement, and the diminutive bird (which is so simple that it is no type and any type of common or garden bird) is in motion, while the large worm which he is heroically tackling provides a coiling counterpoint. To say all this is to overstate to the point of ridicule an utterly straightforward design, and I would not be putting you through this if it was not one of my very favourite patterns. I chose brown as the main colour, with red for the worm and cobalt blue for the banding, as this suits my own rather downbeat tastes; there is no crowd-pleasing going on here ... Indeed it was a dismal seller, and only had a short outing, back in 1997. But I use a small Bird and Worm teapot in this pattern to make tea every single morning. It got broken a few years ago, and without pause or consultation Matthew hastened to have a replacement made, knowing how sad I was. Notwithstanding the resounding commercial unsuccess of this design, I have had a play here with some alternative treatments and uses for this pattern because I love it.

A hymn of praise to the Apple Mac and to Will and Claire, two amazing members of our design team with whom I most often work on design applications. The page opposite is Claire's work and some of my favourite pattern work ever.

I have a bit of a tick about tea; I can't function well without it, and I really like it to be made properly in a teapot, with leaves. I even have a special mixture that I have made up in the tea and coffee shop in the Covered Market in Oxford, equal parts of Ceylon, Lapsang and Earl Grey. The tea maestro in Fortnum & Mason frankly refused to mix these three teas – he made me buy them in separate packets and pronounced dire warnings over the utter wrongness of combining them. But he is in this case much mistaken: the three make a perfect mix, strong enough to need a splash of milk, yet evocative, perfumed, slightly smoky. In the afternoons, when in need of a slightly more bracing tea, I add a Yorkshire tea bag. When I met Matt he declared that he had no time for tea, and I tackled this head on, straight away. I told him that unless he developed a tea habit, or at the very least pretended to, it was no dice. For I depend upon the ritual of early morning tea as one of the very nicest times in the day. And I am happy to say that he considered the matter and acquiesced, and I know that these days he is happy to hang about chatting, sometimes for half an hour, before the press of things he is burning to get on with grows too exigent, and go he must, to the piano, the greenhouse, the kitchen or his desk. Biscuits creep into this cosy and beguiling event, and it's one of the hardest things, in the periodic diets one must endure, to forgo the digestive, or the gingernut. I am really trying to be all Frenchwoman about carbs, to eschew them every day, then manage to make a weekly croissant into a languid event, leaving half of it in the saucer beside my coffee. But it is *hard*! Anyway, as I write, the tea tray comes up with no biscuits. The dogs are awarded one each, while the kettle is boiling, as usual, but that's it.

With a fatal sense of inevitability I can see that I am to return to my least favourite beasts here. Yes, snakes. Because while my teapot clearly bears nothing worse than a common or garden worm about to be bird food, I have to acknowledge that over the years potters have decorated their wares with some very odd things. Do we refer and return helplessly to things we particularly dislike? I can't believe that anyone, not even the strong-stomached French sixteenth-century potter Bernard Palissy, *likes* reptiles, or thinks them evocative of happiness or well-being; surely this is impossible? One of my favourite authors is Barbara Kingsolver; I feel completely in sympathy with her, so it was problematic to realise, while I was reading *The Prodigal Summer*, that much as she obviously loathes snakes, she seems to be compelled to insinuate them into her stories – who can forget the death of the narrator's little sister in the outdoor privy in frankly horrifying circumstances in *The Poisonwood Bible*? Not me, certainly. Perhaps we return to unfavourite things in the hope of overcoming or normalising them, taming the dark creatures which frighten us. Certainly a snake on a plate, no matter how stunningly beautifully and naturalistically rendered, has lost much of its wild power. And of course, its wriggling coils will always offer decorative possibilities – just as my worm shows.

Michael has not inherited any of my horror of reptiles; he loves the natural world in a boyish, un-squeamish way. While we were all eating pizzas at the gates of Herculaneum he spotted a large snake making its slow and frankly horrible way up through the branches of an apple tree – and he wanted to go closer! To see the nasty thing *close up*. As Jack Lemmon pointed out, albeit in different circumstances, it's a whole different sex. Anyway, Mikey took to fishing when we moved to Oxford, where the Thames beckoned enticingly across Port Meadow, and he was keen to spend as much time out there as he possibly could, often

in the company of his cousin Jimmy Joe. At other times he was accompanied
by Martin, a Czech boy who arrived as an au pair and is now an indispensable
friend who has become a truly inspired gardener, a prize-winning ballroom
dancer (he and his sweet girlfriend Daniela are Oxfordshire champions), and
an endlessly good-natured partner in sporting projects for Mikey. Using a trap,
they caught crayfish; then with worms dug in the garden they caught chub and
dace; but the main excitement on Port Meadow was pike. Using lurid lures from
Fat Phil's fishing tackle shop on the Abingdon Road, he and Jimmy landed their
first one, a real whopper, a giant of the dark, and they couldn't stay away from the
river for long after that. There are recent fisherman's stories of monster carp,
whose bait in ever weirder flavours I am always happy to purchase for them.

In Norfolk Mikey goes after trout with his cousin. Edmund is the proof that boys today do *not* all spend their lives glued to the computer: he is an explosives enthusiast, a skilful sportsman, a daring rider of scrambling bikes, and loves mucking about in boats – in short, Michael's hero. Many of these expeditions are early in the morning, or involve a party of school friends, and they do *not* need mums bearing picnics. In fact the likeliest picnic is a pocket full of Tangfastics and a few Peperamis. And I have always encouraged the picnic purchased entirely from Budgens, knowing that squeezy cheese in a white bun, a packet of crisps and a penguin biscuit, if eaten by the river, is pure heaven, and certainly there often isn't time to faff about making elaborate picnics. However, maybe, if I made sausage rolls, Michael, Martin, Edmund or Jimmy would be happy to bung them in their bags with the bait. As long as there was a chocolate biscuit as well.

SAUSAGE ROLLS TO PUT IN THE BAG WITH THE FISHING KIT

You can make these sausage rolls with home-made
or ready-made shortcrust pastry.

Makes 6
550g good-quality pork sausage meat | 6–8 sage leaves, finely chopped
1 teaspoon finely chopped rosemary | 375g puff pastry
1 medium free-range egg, beaten

Put the sausage meat into a bowl and mix in the chopped sage and chopped rosemary. Shape the mixture into two 40cm long sausages.

Roll out the pastry on a lightly floured work surface into a roughly 25 x 35cm rectangle, then cut it in half lengthways. Lay one of the sausages down the middle of each piece of pastry.

Brush one long edge of each strip of pastry with a little beaten egg, then fold the pastry over the sausages so that the edges meet, press them together well, and mark with the tines of a fork. Cut each length into 3 large sausage rolls (or 10 smaller sausage rolls) and make 4 small slits in the top of each one.

Place them on a lightly buttered baking sheet, brush with a little beaten egg and bake at 200°C/180°C Fan/Gas 6 for 25–30 minutes, until crisp and golden.

FRUIT

I have chosen five patterns in each chapter: those shown here are my favourites from a total of about twenty designs inspired by the endlessly pleasing forms of all kinds of fruits, including cherries, blackberries, strawberries, oranges and lemons, pineapples (back in 1997, tiny!), sloes, pomegranates (I first did a formal blue repeating border using a stylised image of this fruit in 1988); also grapes (the Vine pattern in this chapter, and in a very restrained version in 2002) and, most homely, apples and pears.

The decorative allure of bloomy grapes, with their beautiful palmate leaves and twirling tendrils, goes back all the way into the mists of ancient civilisation; as a signifier of plenty and pleasure, the vine is carved, painted, engraved and printed on just about all and every domestic artefact you can think of, from glasses and bowls, table linen and furnishing fabrics to furniture and panelling. I feel pleased with my early Vine pattern, mostly because I didn't agonise over it, I just sat down and drew it one day in 1988 and as a result it has a flow and simplicity that suits the subject. In 1990 we put a pattern called Olives into the catalogue, which proved a bigger hit commercially. I think that as a simple border it is especially easy to use, as all food looks good on it.

In the spring of 2006 Matthew and I went to stay outside Rome for a long weekend; we had a lovely time, looked at churches, wandered through markets and ate lots of delicious food, but we were also on a mission: we wanted to try to get a handle on the notion of La Dolce Vita. So we walked among the vines and olives thinking about the balmy, easy weather, the deep and fertile soil, the gently rolling fields and woods which constitute the conditions in which civilisation reached (so long ago!) such a peachy perfection; an ideal way of life which was so commanding that we are all still fascinated by it to the point of obsession. We talked about the deep love affair with the Mediterranean conducted by all contemporary cooks, most definitely including ourselves, and pondered on the comfort of southern softness for the northern soul, as it has evolved in its long dark cold winters. We were sure that a winning design should be all about olives and grapes, the quintessential produce of Italy. But you know, the more sure we felt about this, the more elusive the idea seemed – we wanted to say much more than just a border of olives and grapes entwined – and we went home feeling frustrated. Which is what we deserved, perhaps for trying to define and own such a beautiful and nebulous idea: La Dolce Vita is to be courted and charmed, long sought and perhaps only really earned by those people who don't bother themselves with suits and mobile phones, but simply take up a scythe – and learn how to use it with ease and grace, all day long.

So it was that when we sat down in our office in Norfolk to come up with a new Mediterranean-inspired design we found that we had quickly to put aside the (beautiful!) sketches that Matt had laboured over in Italy, and think about what we really knew. And what emerged was the pattern called Kitchen Garden, based on all the fun we were having making one, right outside the window of the office.

The Marmalade pattern from 2013, with its slices of big juicy February Spanish oranges, and also Pomegranates, which emerged as a special for the publishing company, Persephone Books in the same year 2012, works because, as with the Vine pattern from so long ago, I didn't agonise or over-think, I just sat down and drew the fruits themselves, planning a generous large-scale pattern in glowing colours.

Vine

When we quit Norfolk for Oxfordshire in 2009, Matt and I often discussed – sometimes jokingly and sometimes almost with dread – our fears that we were turning our back on an idyll, and exchanging the robust rural values of a settled community for what must be, given its proximity to London, a severely compromised way of life, with cars probably bumper to bumper, scarcely a car park between supermarkets, no sign of a barn owl and no room for the type of men who drive pick-ups held together with baler twine. These anxieties were heightened by friends who felt, who still feel passionately, that it is incontrovertible: in the south of England we all live stressed lives with no time to lean on gates looking at the view, and they are un-picturesque gates to boot, chained up to deter gypsies and fly-tipping, and revealing landscapes scarred with roads, industrial estates and ugly housing developments. They were on their way to Norfolk, said the friends, last outpost of real life …

And what we learned was this: it takes a little bit of time to be accepted into any community, even in the more mobile counties, but if you open your eyes, and stop to say hello, if you commit to using local builders and to shopping in the village (if you are lucky enough to have a village shop, not always the case, I know), and if you buy the Ordnance Survey maps of your area and use them to explore – then like us you will almost certainly be surprised, delighted even. We tried to tell our sceptical friends this, but they still disbelieve, alas.

Our village is wonderful, really an amazing community, but I refuse to believe that it is exceptional. This is what we found. Yes, the land we bought had been rather brutally treated: we have planted hundreds of trees and put in lots of hedges, cleared ditches and left rough the marshy areas to improve the wildlife prospects; meanwhile, all around us, in walking distance, there are many remarkable landscapes, with meadows and woods and Neolithic tumps. We swim in the rivers and picnic in the meadows, and they are teeming with wildlife – barn owls, kestrels, finches, swallows, swifts, and even grass snakes are plentiful. (Oh dear, it seems that I am compelled to bring snakes into almost every chapter, in this case as proof that all is in fact right with the world.)

Almost without exception we buy all our supplies in the Co-op in the village marketplace, where on Thursdays a fish van sells delicious wares, and newspapers are available from 6 a.m. from a caravan. Sometimes at nights a pizza oven is set up, and the kebab van is almost a fixture, so apart from a hardware supplies in a nearby village, a wine dealer in another, and some trips to the Covered Market in Oxford for exotic dietary additions, we don't

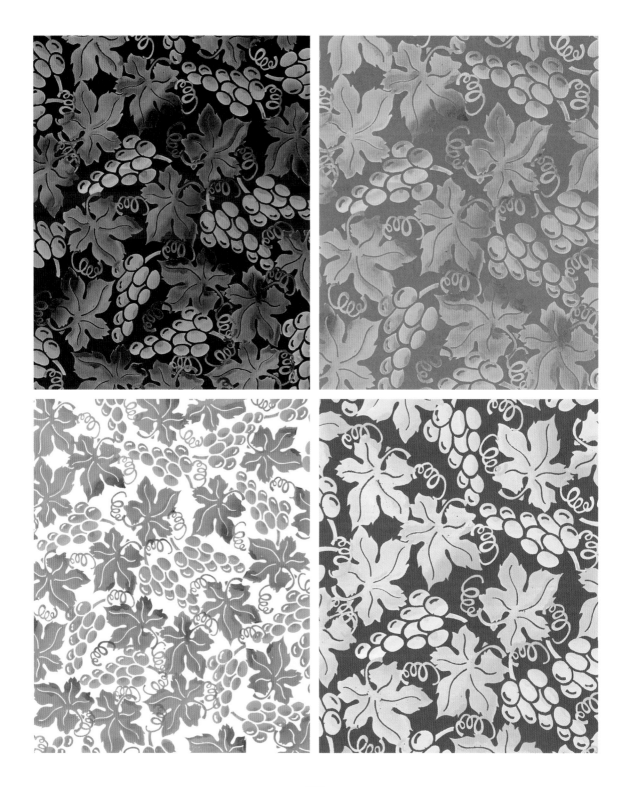

feel hemmed in by supermarkets and manage almost never to use them. Yes, there are far too many enormous new cars, but that's life, and there are, oh joy, *plenty* of rackety old vehicles, many of them often drawn up in our yard on earth-moving or game-keeping affairs. Or I buy them: I'm in love with my white Capri – it's perfect for a night out at the circus, and ideal for making friends in low places.

And what, pray, has all this to do with vines? I'm coming to that. When we moved into the village our nearest neighbour was an extraordinary man called Roy. He had lived in the village all his life, with some years away in the Merchant Navy, and some more during the war when he took part in the Anzio landings. His ensuing adventures gave him a lifelong love of Italy, and when years later his son worked as a long-distance lorry driver, Roy often went with him; and from one such trip he brought home some vine cuttings from Tuscany. They (like every other plant) thrived in his beautiful garden.

Kelmscott, the home of William and Janey Morris, is about three miles upriver from our favourite swimming place. Matt and I often walk there along the river path, which is also an inspiring approach to this, the heart of the Arts and Crafts Movement.

When Roy died the large village church was packed full and the whole village mourned him and told wonderful stories, including his love of family picnics and fishing expeditions in the meadows all around the village. He was the epitome of a real English countryman, one who stood for all and more that we had feared might be disappearing from southern England. And he had brought home to Bampton from Italy the final touch of evolved, settled, civilised rural life – a vine. The vine is the simplest and the strongest and most essential way of illustrating classical southern ease, warmth, hospitality and abundance. He gave Matthew some cuttings, and they are now growing in our yard.

When I drew the vine pattern all of this was in the future. But it is true to say that it was one of my first patterns because I wanted to illustrate on my domestic wares, in a simple way, all the really important things in life. So I chose the plants that embody my deepest convictions when drawing my first free-form patterns: Roses for the glory of summer, Figs for voluptuous meals, Chestnut Leaves for permanence, Lilies for glamour, Morning Glory for kitchen gardens and the Vine for welcome.

APRICOTS POACHED IN VIN SANTO

Served just warm, these apricots make an ideal
end to lunch under a trellis on a hot summer day.

Serves 8
500ml Vin Santo (Italian sweet wine) | 200g light soft brown sugar
1 vanilla pod, split open lengthways | 1 star anise
Pared zest of 2 lemons
600g fresh apricots, halved and stones removed

Put the Vin Santo, sugar, vanilla pod, star anise and lemon zest into a pan with
100ml of water and slowly bring to the boil, stirring to dissolve the sugar.

Add the halved apricots and simmer gently for 1 minute, or until they can
be pierced easily with a cocktail stick. This will depend on their ripeness, so
keep an eye on them, as they can soften very fast.

Lift the fruit with a slotted spoon into a serving bowl. Return the pan
of syrup to the heat and boil rapidly until reduced by half. Add the juice of
1 lemon, then strain back over the fruit and serve warm, or chill until needed.

Rosehip

It occurred to me this morning, while I was putting on my shoes beside a teetering pile of the books I'm reading at the moment, that I might have read more words than I have ever spoken: it seems when I look back at my childhood that I spent a lot of time reading about the things I wished I was doing. Ponies in particular: I knew pretty much the complete works of Ruby Ferguson, Joanna Cannan and her daughters Josephine, Christine and Diana Pullein-Thompson, not to mention Pat Smythe, Primrose Cumming and K. M. Peyton. More than all of these I loved *The Ponies of Bunts*, *National Velvet*, *My Friend Flicka*, *The Far Distant Oxus*, *Moorland Mousie* and, best of all, *The Irish RM*. But I never had a pony of my own. I don't want to sound pathetic – I had loads of fun on other children's ponies, and spent summers riding bareback around Bassingbourn with my friend Posy; I looked after a lovely dapple grey pony called Pius for a sixth-former at my school and loved riding in the villages on the edge of Oxford: Elsfield, Beckley, Stanton St John. Thanks to my heavenly aunt Theresa I also did lots of hunting, in Cornwall and in Northumberland: I was always being run away with, I had some big falls, whichever pony I was riding frequently lay down to cool off in a stream, dunking me unceremoniously, or bucked me off, or kicked other riders or, worst of all, a hound. Most of my time out hunting was actually spent scrambling and staggering after my steed as it galloped embarrassingly about the field, head up, stirrups and reins flying, and I was really very hopeless – but always very enthusiastic.

One summer Theresa organised a thrilling two-day ride fifty miles across Northumberland. Riding mostly over open moor and woodland, stopping to swim and picnic on the way, we imagined ourselves as fleeing from border rievers or Roman legions – it felt heroic and ancient.

The days of pony obsession, whether chasing for ages around the field trying inexpertly to catch a naughty pony, or at worryingly close quarters if I fell off as it shied and dumped me painfully into a thorny place – these were the times, I think, when I first made real contact with the world of outdoors, and for some reason I always noticed and loved hedges from this time onwards. Out hunting, thrilled and appalled by jumping, I noticed closely how varied were these fearsome obstacles, tall and whippy, or thick and neatly laid; solid enough to feel warm out of the wind behind me, and full of treacherous

thorns (the blackthorns are poisonous for rider and pony alike, and are very sore until picked out with tweezers and smeared with mag. sulph.). Hedges were a sturdy feature.

Put another way, the single biggest effect of pony life was the time – the days and weeks spent out of doors in all weather, noticing the appalling smell of the billy-goat put out with his cattle by the Cornish farmer to avert abortion amongst his cows; seeing a just-hatched adder family wriggling in the glare of a stony track; joggling around the roads out exercising in horizontal rain; trekking across the moors and through the forestry in north Northumberland, plagued by flies in sweltering heat, stopping to plunge into a stream: all those aeons of time spent outside meant that nature seeped and sometimes flooded into me, and thereafter I have just always been aware of it all, of crops, tracks, gates, fences, birds, animals, wildflowers, trees and hedges.

Hedges provide a panorama of seasonal change. Early in the year the bleak black empty branches start to shade into purple. Then, just when some early warm days have made us all think of spring, comes the Blackthorn Winter. This was my great-aunt Pen's name for the cold blast of weather which often accompanies the flowering of the blackthorn in the hedges in March. Then the hawthorn, whose heavenly blossom in May smells of the very essence of the dread and the elation of exams. As the summer progresses the field maple comes into leaf, an extraordinarily lovely red for a few days; and in June the wild roses throw their arching sprays of palest pink flowers abundantly all about. In autumn sloes, haws and rosehips create endless material for my teacher Miss Niblett and her nature-table still-lifes. I know that books shaped these emotions as well: I have declared before my love and admiration for Ladybird books, a favourite of my redoubtable but twinkly-eyed first teacher at Oxford High. I still have shelves of them, and the series called What to Look For ..., illustrated by the great Charles Tunnicliffe, is richly inspiring and hugely nostalgic.

In the very early months of my business I filled sketchbooks with ideas for and notes about pottery decoration. Among these inexpert drawings I see that, it being autumn, I made several attempts to convey some of these deep feelings. I drew hawthorns and sloes (which I came back to later to make into another pattern) and also rosehips. And while this was not among my earliest designs, I had this theme in mind from the start. Rosehip (1999) was only a moderate success, but I like it very much, so I have done some experiments with it here, just in case they might be useful. I am perfectly certain that this pattern is from my drawings; Matthew is equally sure that he did them. I have no idea who is right. Rosehip was preceded by a rather similar pattern called Blackberries in 1997.

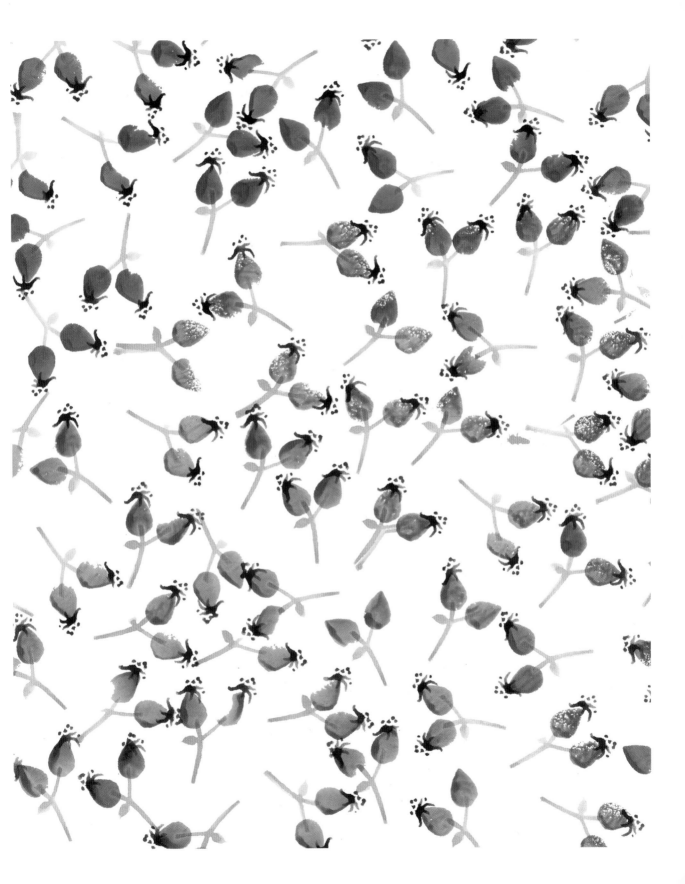

Pomegranates

Retail: it's all about a knockout display. And of course about one hundred other things, but making the merchandise desirable is the key to making the tills ring. I first understood this in Brixton Market years ago, where the simple fact that all the hardware was displayed in such jolly profusion meant that I always came home with a washing-up bowl, a waste-paper basket or some new loo brushes, whether we needed them or not, simply because all these things, the very least aspirational goods I can imagine, were sold out of displays made from enormous quantities of stock. In England in general we only use this technique in sale time, and in greengrocers. Bonners, in Oxford's Covered Market, always have beautiful, bountiful displays. Harvest Festival in church was always an embarrassment; if they couldn't make it look as lush as Bonners, I wondered, why do it? I have since found some challenges to their pre-eminence in display skills; the first was in Austin, Texas.

This is a town so well worth visiting that if I was not able to drive I would be prepared to walk there all the way from New York, if only to visit its bars, record stores and vintage clothing emporiums; to see the bats coming in to roost at dusk under the South Congress Avenue Bridge, and to stay in the Austin Motel or indeed the San José Hotel, which are both top places. On a trip there with the family we were advised by a breakfast waitress that we would love the store called Whole Foods. Now you may have visited their shop in Kensington High Street, but please just set that to one side, as this was truly the *Texan* version. For Austin, the ultimate alternative city, whose green and Eco credentials stand in utter counterpoint to the glorious vast excesses of this, the most rambunctious state in the USA, is still in all important ways Texan to the core. And the great thing about Texas is that everything is outsize: the chicken-fried chicken portions as well as the steaks, the welcome, the choice in cowboy boots, the acreage of the great ranches, the venom of the scorpions and rattlesnakes, the *trucks* – and the displays in Whole Foods. When we walked into the Austin Whole Foods store we felt like refugees from a time of rationing, dumbstruck by the plenty. The minced meats came in enormous skeins, like b-i-i-i-i-g balls of pink wool, and these skeins were piled twenty deep. The steaks were out of the world of the Flintstones, the sausage display would have fed every scout ever sworn in, the ice cream aisle went on out of sight – and that was probably just displaying the variations on vanilla. There was practically a city of ice cream choice. It was jaw-dropping, and incredibly beautiful, brightly coloured, as artfully lit as Garbo; the fruit and veg all misted with beads of condensation and the freshest fish ever seen, all piled up

and nestled among diamond pure ice crystals ... Kitty's remark was: 'Mumma, I swear that they have been inventing new kinds of fruit in here.' We could only sigh faintly in utter agreement.

There may have been pomegranates in Austin, I can't remember. But when we went to stay for a week in the old city of Damascus, just three or four months before Syria plunged into civil war, the displays in the marvellous old Al-Hamidiyah Souk were in another dimension. And not just the food, but the displays of *everything* were eye-popping, from pony harness (what colour tassels?) to fishing nets (like an illustrated bible scene); to underwear with the strangest and wildest decorations, the most acceptable example of which I can remember was of embroidered birds and blossoms. The underwear fell

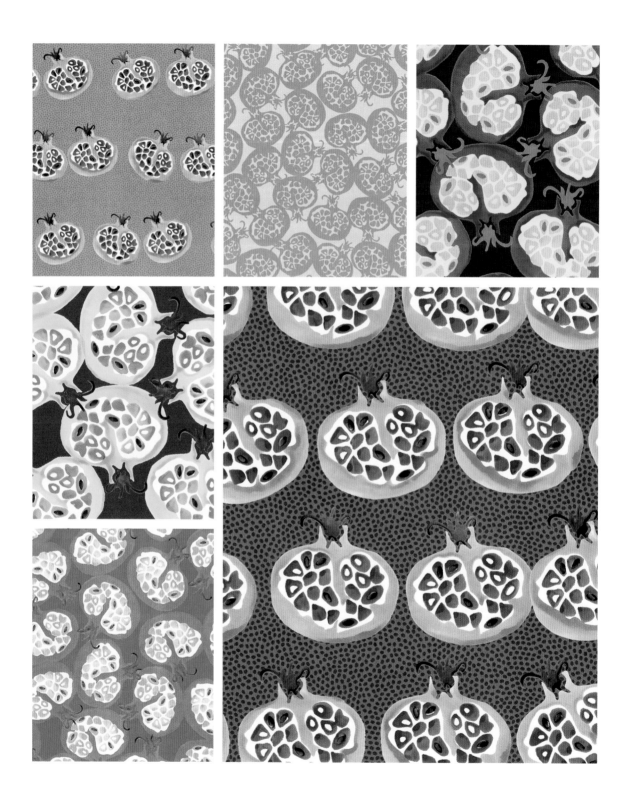

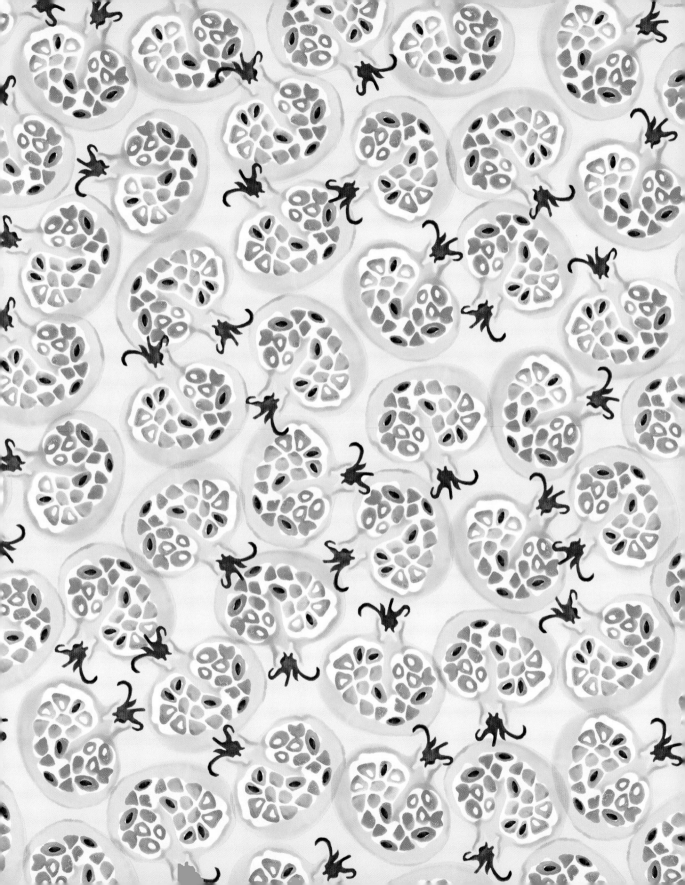

magically to the floor when you clapped your hands … (truly, I'm not making this up!) We wandered outside the souk through whole streets selling nothing but olives, which were piled into hundreds and hundreds of enormous black rubber dishes, four feet across, made from recycled lorry tyres. The incredible din, especially in the metalworkers' halls and the streets outside the souk, amplified the feeling of teeming life, huge numbers of mouths to feed, and all in incredibly cheerful but grimy conditions. As well as harness and fishing nets (tremendously heavy on account of the hundreds of lead weights!) we also bought spices, of course, and carpets, and scarves, and Matt longed passionately for a kitchen, so that we could buy fresh food and cook it. He lusted after the knobbly peppers, and onions of all shapes and sizes; he badly wanted to be slicing those tomatoes, sloshing oils out of beautiful tins, and sprinkling showers of the exotic herbs whose profusion made us long to roll in them, like the dogs do when you lay new carpet.

But of course we were staying in a hotel. So instead we fell on the street stalls and ate delicious houmous, olives, yoghurt with mint, and imam bayildi, from little red pottery bowls (or, more often, plastic ones), or stopped at a window to buy flatbread peeled off the outside of the great humpy oven, slicked with a few drops of oil and sprinkled with za'atar for instant consumption. We went also to a bigger baking set-up, where the men (who spoke, so our fabulous guide Malika told us, Aramaic) had finished the day's bread-making and were cooking trays of aubergines for the whole neighbourhood in the last of the ovens' heat. The trays were all over the street for cooling before collection and the aubergines were the most glamorous silvery-greyish deep purple, like roasted breasts of birds of paradise might look.

But while Matt was poring over the veg, I found the fruit, and at last got the hang of pomegranates. I had read the myth in childhood, about Demeter, Persephone and Hades; and while so many of the stories of the ancient gods slide away, and don't stick in my imagination, this story has deep resonance combined with simple clout. It speaks of fertility and our utter dependence on the power of the natural world – huge arching themes leading to ancient magic rites and superstitions; and at the same time of very human feelings: maternal love and fury. At the heart of the story, Persephone shows the weakness in us, the simple giving-in to temptation – with rather massive consequences. And the confusion only used to come in at this point for me, because I couldn't see pomegranates as tempting; the only ones I came across before Damascus were wizened and battered, with only baffling little dry-ish pips, buried in pith, which didn't seem worth the fiddly task involved in extracting a small bowl of them. The taste, after all the peeling, struck me as faintly like shampoo, and generally not in the least bit tempting. But here in the souk they were fresh and completely different, with bright skins and jewel-like scarlet pips bursting with a juice whose combination of scented sweetness and sharp dry lemony tang seemed to be exactly what you would pine for. I could imagine Persephone's long dry trudge through ashy and sulphurous tunnels on the way out of the Underworld, and I could understand exactly how she felt drawn to swallow just a tiny handful, thinking no one would know. Thanks to Yotam Ottolenghi, the thrilling stories of the food of the Middle East have suddenly jumped into our kitchens: along with za'atar, tahini, tamarind, rose water and clouds of pink sumac, it turns out that scatterings of pomegranate seeds, and a spoonful of pomegranate syrup, are now everyday ingredients.

NELL'S FLATBREAD

Nell's flatbread with cumin seeds is delicious for serving with houmous (see recipe on page 215) or indeed with imam bayildi or taramasalata.

Makes 24

1 tablespoon dried active yeast | 500g strong plain white or wholemeal flour
1 tablespoon cumin seeds | $\frac{3}{4}$ teaspoon fine sea salt
50ml extra virgin olive oil

Whisk the dried active yeast into 300ml of warm water and set aside somewhere warm for about 5 minutes, until the surface is covered in a thick layer of foam.

Sift the flour into a bowl and stir in the cumin seeds and sea salt. Make a well in the centre and add the yeasty mixture and the extra virgin olive oil. Mix together into a dough, turn out on to a lightly floured work surface, and knead for about 5 minutes until smooth and elastic. Drop into a clean, lightly oiled bowl, cover with a clean tea towel and leave somewhere warm for 45 minutes to 1 hour, to rise and double in size.

Uncover the bowl, knock back the dough, then put it back on the work surface and knead briefly once more until smooth. Divide the dough into approximately 24 ping-pong size (35g) balls. Roll each one out thinly into an oval flatbread measuring about 9 x 14cm.

Heat a dry heavy-based frying pan over a medium-high heat. Cook the flatbreads 2 at a time for 2 minutes, then flip them over and cook for a further 3 minutes, until they are cooked through and both sides are marked with brown spots. Wrap them in a clean tea towel while you cook the rest.

Kitchen Garden

When Matt and I sat down to plan this pattern in 2006 we thought we had nailed a new take on Portmeirion's Botanic Garden. Well. That plot completely *failed*, as the pattern sold only mildly. Then, instead of working at it, as I know we always should, taking the elements that were slightly more successful and working on them to strengthen the design, we hastily withdrew the pattern and forgot all about it. But the theme is a good one, surely? In fact I know that it is. I think that I simply got the slightly offbeat text wrong: the suggestions sound to my ear now just a bit offhand, where they were intended to be encouraging, mildly thought-provoking, or simply to remind you of something you might have forgotten. Moreover, there was not enough pattern coverage, which left too much bare space. But Matthew's illustrations of fruit are beautiful and well worth revisiting one day.

We were deeply immersed at the time in creating a big kitchen garden at Wickmere. We were bubbling with all the questions this raised about designing and achieving the perfect version, including the speedy creation of shelter, the positioning of tanks, taps, trees – also *varieties* – that burning issue for this generation of gardeners. Not to forget paths, poultry control, a greenhouse, an outdoor cooking arrangement and compost heaps.

I don't think that all these things were so vital to previous generations of normal-scale gardeners. Surely there was just a veg patch and that was that? Plus maybe a couple of gooseberry bushes, and a gnarled old apple tree leaning at an angle.

During most of the 1939–45 war, Granny and Granfa were in the Sudan (as it then was). He was in the Political Service, an outpost of Empire considered to be particularly testing and rather dashing in the 1920s, when he joined after he came down from Cambridge with a double first in Classics. Granny went too, because like many of her contemporaries she weighed the relative duties of wife and mother and seemed untroubled by her decision to put her husband's needs before those of her children. It's hard to get under the skin of these events in my family's past: they loom large, but they were not discussed. Granny once complained sadly to me that it was a source of pain and puzzlement to them that their children and grandchildren would never talk about his work in the Sudan. As I remember it, the shaming collapse of the great adventure and mission of Empire, just as soon as it was packed up, was an unofficially embargoed subject, rarely if ever talked about, privately or nationally. Equally we never really heard what it was like for my mother and uncle to see neither parent for most of the duration of the war.

Instead, we grew up knowing that Mum had a great love for Granny's sister Penelope, known to us always as Aunt Pen (even though she was of course our great-aunt), who took on the largest share of their care in this period. Aunt Pen was definitely not of the soft and twinkly type – she was, instead, from the tribe of splendid and eccentric aunts. To my siblings and me she was a daunting visitor, whose arrival was slightly to be feared; and she came to stay frequently, as Mum was understandably devoted to her. She would turn up in her battered Cortina estate with her miniature dachshund; the last one was called Phoebe. Phoebe did tricks: she jumped over Aunt Pen's ankles as she sang The Keel Row (Aunt P, that is, not the dog), and she Died for King and Country, which we longed for, and chorused for, though there was a terrible danger of getting the giggles.

If you love vegetable gardens, I strongly recommend to you the *Potager du Roi* at Versailles. Tour the palace, walk out to the Trianon, then find a café and eat something delicious, as you will be faint from the splendours and excesses as well as the mileage.

Aunt Pen always looked straight at one, and spoke exactly as she found, which could be withering, since she found us undisciplined and too noisy. But beneath an austere exterior she was warm and loving, and when she checked herself into a convent nursing home in Chiswick so as not to be a burden to her nieces, she was near enough to come to lunch often with Matt and me in Fulham, and she was totally game for a picnic in Chiswick House in all weather. I found it moving that she was losing her grip on speech just as our first daughter, Lizzy, was starting to talk. She looked down one day, delighted by Lizzy dressing up to go for a walk after lunch, and said, 'Darling, what smart ... smart ... red things you have there.' And Lizzy supplied, 'They're gum boots, Aunt Pen.'

When she was staying she liked, and Mum encouraged her, to have breakfast in bed, and her frequent requests for 'A little stewed apple if you are passing, dear' from behind her open bedroom door have lived on as a loving family joke. And it is entirely her fault that I am so addicted to stewed apple. To me it is as all-powerful a cure as chicken soup is for other folk. As I child I spent much time at the kitchen table, often beside Aunt Pen, peeling, coring and slicing apples for stewing. She was utterly imbued with parsimony, and was very sharp about cutting away too much of the core, leading to the outcry: 'Yuck, there are toenails in the apple.' In turn I make my children do this – without toenails, please.

Thus a part of me knows, thanks to Aunt Pen, that I could get by with a modest veg patch as long as I have apple trees. But I am so impressed by, and very deeply grateful for Matthew's extraordinary skill and energy in gardening, which means that I always have a veg and fruit selection of perfect beauty and quality, and a vegetable garden far superior to any I can think of. At home we need a thousand ways to dispose of the wonderfully abundant tomatoes from Matt's vegetable garden. One of my favourites is a salad with tomato, burrata, pesto and pine nut kernels. This is only worth making if you can lay your hands on high-quality burrata and fancy heritage tomatoes – I mean it! Other recent crazes include tomato soup – hardly original, but so adaptable and delicious – and baked tomatoes on toast for breakfast.

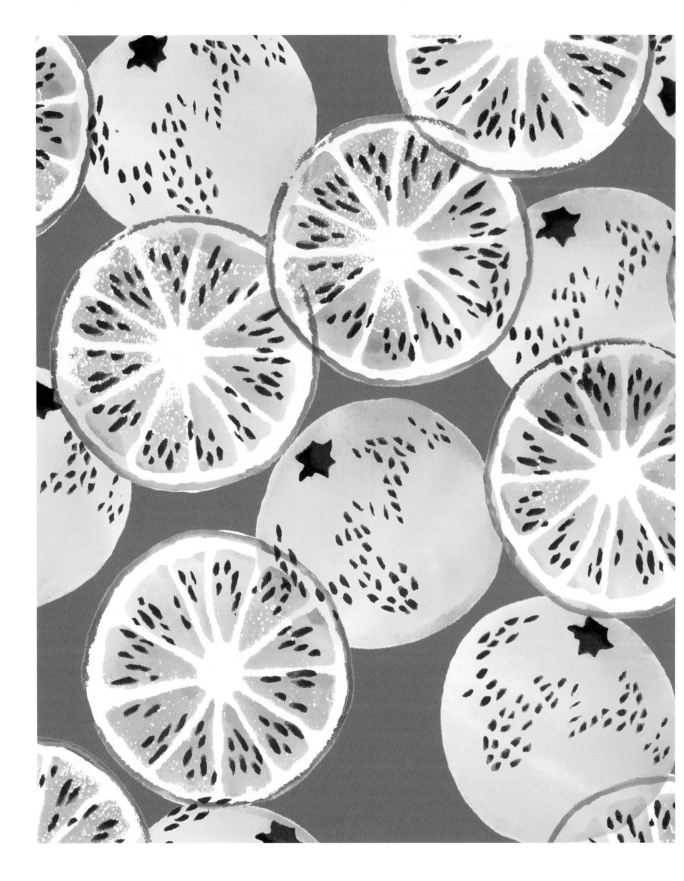

Marmalade

For the purposes of this chapter, cast out the image of the jam pan and instead think of oranges. I want you to imagine citrus-coloured Mary Quant mini dresses with wet-look patent white boots. Focus on the carefree moment in about 1970 when life was cheerier; it cost less, and it was coloured very vividly, often in deep orange. The fashion was thrilling and the cars were smaller, tinnier and they often broke down. Thumbing a lift was normal, Mum and Rick often picked up hitch-hikers in our orange Volkswagen. Actually I can't think of one single notion which more perfectly gives you the whole difference between those free-wheeling years and our anxious age: when did you last stop to pick up a stranger on the road? No. I thought not.

My uncle, Martin, has always been a figure of total glamour to me; he sailed to win, and still does; he surfed standing up on a Malibu board off the Cornish beaches in the sixties when such exploits were almost unheard of. When I was little he was always surrounded by beautiful girls and dashing friends, all about to go and win point-to-point races, or drive to Marrakesh. Martin rented a ramshackle farm on Bodmin Moor. The moor is a remote place with a mossy, mysterious character. However, a visit to Martin's landlords Robin and Marika across the valley offered a culture shock – their house would have suited James Bond if he fancied hiding away in Cornwall.

My hazy memories of this house in 1970 conjure huge rooms with low white sofas and chairs in the distance. We were always muddy, and I was in awe of the mess we might make. There were brightly coloured carpets, and cushions in turquoise, pink and orange. The house was full of the sort of black metal furniture, often tiled, capable of inflicting grievous wounds. It was pure contemporary glamour with a hard edge, and it fascinated and unnerved me. They were a wild couple: as well as big noisy drinks parties they loved games such as hare and hounds, but over long courses with scary tests such as high rope ladders and long, steep death-slides.

Marika was an accomplished cook, and her kitchen was absolutely nothing like any I'd ever been in: it was huge, white, and full of shiny surfaces and all the latest gadgets. She was a generous supporter of Martin's fledgling business: he smoked mackerel, principally to sell to pubs whose food offering at that time was usually not more than a bag of salted crisps. Marika did the kind of exhibition cookery that Mum did not, and I was loyally slightly disapproving, but looking back I can see that she was totally admirable, a trail blazer in the food world. I like the memory of her gravelly laugh even though I always tried to wriggle out of spending a night there, as it was not a cosy place to wake in the dark.

PORK & LIVER TERRINE

Serves 10–12

1 tablespoon olive oil | 175g (approx. 4 large) shallots, finely chopped
100g streaky bacon, roughly chopped | 175g pig's liver, cut into small pieces
500g minced belly pork | 225g good-quality pork sausage meat
1 medium free-range egg, beaten
The finely grated zest and juice of 1 small orange
3 tablespoons chopped fresh thyme leaves
2 tablespoons chopped fresh sage leaves
1½ teaspoons salt | 1 teaspoon freshly ground black pepper

To decorate
3 small fresh bay leaves | 2 small orange slices (halved if you wish)
1 x 400g tin of beef consommé | 1 tablespoon (1 sachet) gelatine powder
3–4 small sprigs of fresh thyme | 12 black peppercorns

Heat the olive oil in a small pan, add the chopped shallots and fry gently until they are soft but not browned. Tip into a large mixing bowl and leave to cool.

Put the streaky bacon into a food processor and coarsely chop, using the pulse button. Add it to the bowl of shallots. Put the liver into the processor and again, coarsely chop and add to the bowl, together with the minced belly pork, pork sausage meat, beaten egg, orange zest and juice, thyme, sage, salt and pepper. Mix together well with your hands.

Pack the mixture into a 1.2 litre terrine dish or loaf tin and press the bay leaves and 2 halved orange slices on to the surface. Cover securely with a lid or some lightly oiled foil, put into a small roasting tin, and pour boiling water into the tin until it comes halfway up the sides of the dish/tin. Bake at 180°C/160°C Fan/Gas 4 for 1½ hours. Remove and leave to cool.

You now need to weight the terrine overnight. The easiest way to do this is to cut out a piece of cardboard that will fit inside the rim of the dish/tin. Cover it with foil, rest it on top of the terrine and weight it down. If you have another dish/tin of the same size, place this on top and fill it with anything heavy.

To decorate the top of the terrine, pour the consommé into a small pan, sprinkle over the gelatine powder and leave it to 'sponge' for 5 minutes. Heat gently until clear, then leave to cool. Arrange the thyme sprigs and pepper-corns among the bay leaves and orange slices, pour over the consommé, and leave it to chill in the fridge overnight. Serve cut into slices, with cornichons and fresh bread.

THE SEA

Whether traipsing along the marshes complaining about Granny's sand-shoes edict (we had to wear them *all* the time, even when they were wet and annoying and uncomfortable after a session of mudlarking in Morston Creek, but we longed to run around with bare feet) or experimenting with different gilly crab bait (bacon rinds, uncooked, and a chicken drumstick are both excellent), it is an ingrained habit to remember the weather of my childhood Norfolk summer holidays as always sunny. But of course, it wasn't. In fact, the last two weeks of August last year, also spent in north Norfolk, were a fairly typical, chilly holiday, during which we did swim and picnic, but not very much – in fact we spent quite a lot of time indoors, reading, watching films and planning trips, then not stirring further than Holt, or maybe to Wells for fish and chips. These are the peaceful luxuries which arrive as one's children become languid, good-natured teenagers; smaller children drive their parents to find activities, without which they will kill them with the awful sound of ragging (that is, rolling about like puppies), which turns into fighting, which leads to shrieking ... Wet afternoons can last for ever under these trying conditions: what to do?

On such afternoons, Mum sometimes favoured the Shell Museum at Glandford, just inland from Blakeney. Looking at the building now, I find it hard to imagine that we quietened down for long, but of course, as is always the case, she took us there because she loved it, and while I didn't fully appreciate the place when I was little, I came to love it dearly. This is a little inlaid treasure box of a building, as perfect in its way as the church of the Miracoli in Venice, was custom-built by Sir Alfred Jodrell in about 1900 to house the collection of shells and other curiosities belonging to him and his sisters. Then, as now, my main interest lay in the bouquets and baskets, the birds and flowers made from shells and displayed like beautiful cakes under glass domes. Sir Alfred also put his eccentric stamp on the little church which stands just above the museum: the building is lined with carved panelling, full of unselfconscious love and energy.

The Glandford Shell Museum is a perfectly expanded cabinet of curiosities, just as the Pitt Rivers Museum in Oxford is a vast version of the same thing: Granny had implanted in us a total understanding of this phenomenon when she gave each of us when young a Sunday Box, encouraging us thereafter to make our own mini ethnographic collections of favourite tiny things, always including favourite shells from memorable beaches.

One way or another, Norfolk flavours my life and my designs pretty strongly, as these stories indicate, and I am always happy when images of its beaches and marshes come into my mind – I think we all have a little burst of happiness at the evocation of seaside holidays, don't you? This makes seaside themes promising for design material.

Coral

The pattern called simply Coral is one I did in the early days, in 1985. It was inspired by a very tattered and torn cover on an old nursery chair in an outlying bedroom of a house I used to stay in for parties. The design has always carried for me an atmosphere of the faded, forgotten and forlorn; I love all these qualities, and, like the hero of *Le Grand Meaulnes* at the makeshift party in the mysterious abandoned house, I know that I'm always looking for something marvellous which is very close, but always just out of reach. Meanwhile consolation is to be found in the broken remnants of a past not fully understood, but throbbing with love and loss. Which pretty much defines my teenage sensibilities.

I was passionately romantic, and never happier than when exploring old attics, sheds and barns in search of treasure. In the loft above the coach house (a magic formula!) of the old rectory that Granny and Granfa bought in north Northumberland in about 1972, I found, and in the dusty half-light sat down to read, piles of old illustrated children's encyclopaedias. There were mouse-nibbled magazines from 1910, and piles of broken leather-bound books whose endpapers of tiny-scale, reticulated patterns in shades of brown chimed quietly with the chair cover when I first saw it a year or two later. These in turn felt like the foxed engravings of seaweeds and mosses which hung on the stairs to the bachelor quarters, the rooms for single male guests around the billiard-room, in another fading house.

In these days of hedge-funded super-wealth, the shabby and the faded are under serious threat and I dearly love visiting a house which has *not* had the usual makeover, where 40-watt bulbs cast dim shadows down creaking passages to bathrooms with cracked lino on the floor and a huge rust-stained bath never to know really hot water; where dead flies accumulate among the crisp pleats of shredded curtains and Kodachrome photos of the first summer of the swimming pool fade to yellow under the glass of the dressing table. We are being invaded by the look of the boutique hotel: resistance is very important.

Like seaweeds and mosses, corals are a perfect starting point for any designer in any medium who is looking to cover surfaces with an abstracted pattern that pleases the eye, soothes the harshness of blank expanses, strikes a dignified but pleasing note with a natural resonance without making a distraction. The point of these types of corally patterns is that they are never a threat to the main event; they only enrich, they never detract.

If I return to the upholstered chair which was the direct parent of my pattern: the long-gone lady who chose that chintz never saw chair covers as a

subject of conversation, I think. Similarly, the publishers who bound their histories and biographies in fine calfskin with mossy printed paper linings didn't dream of a world where the endpapers of a book might actually become the chief selling-point of that work. Since ancient times builders have chosen to vermiculate the stone of lower storeys of a building constructed out of dressed stone above, precisely so that we accept the solidity and antiquity of a temple or palace without conscious thought – this beautiful mazy carving reproducing the action on stone over millennia of nameless deep sea creatures is never noted or commented upon, it is just there. This simplicity seems almost unbelievably luxurious, don't you think?

> Now Matthew says that I am confused, that big buildings with vermiculated lower storeys are anything but shy and retiring. But I think that my point holds, that this carving, representing thousands of unacknowledged man-hours, is taken for granted in a way which amounts to the modest understatement that this type of detailing represents.

Along with overhead bulbs, the bathroom down the passage, apple stores, the hotplate on the sideboard, wooden porridge bowls, telephone directories, fur coats and SodaStream machines, we have also pretty much lost the knack of nursery food. I have a friend who is married to a noted cook – exponent of delicious and modish dishes and thrower of fantastic parties, she is inspired and inspiring, yet still he pines for nursery food and speaks with resigned sadness of poached chicken, rissoles, and most of all, he sighs longingly, for *fish in sauce*. This is now only available, as far as I know, in Wiltons, where, incidentally, it comes with a thrilling wealth of silver cruets and starchy napery, phalanxes of comfortingly strict ancient waiters and even lemons in little muslin covers. You used to be able to rely on the Garrick Club for unfashionable food such as stew with dumplings, followed, like the procession of the equinoxes, by Queen of Puddings, but they revamped the decor and the kitchen at the same time and now you wish faintly for dark glasses to protect you from the dazzlingly restored pictures, all aflame in their brightly gilded frames, while you eat your (delicious!) pumpkin ravioli.

So if you have ancient uncles, or old-fashioned friends, coming to dinner you will not be disappointed by their reaction to this recipe: fish in (palest) pink sauce with very buttery mashed potatoes and green beans. Follow it with a favourite old-fashioned treat such as Guards' Pudding.

FISH IN PINK SAUCE

Serves 6

2.5 litres fresh fish stock (ideally home-made)

6 x 175–200g pieces of thick, unskinned cod loin or fillet

(ideally cut from just behind the head, where it is thickest)

60g butter | 60g plain flour | 1–2 teaspoons freshly squeezed lemon juice

2 teaspoons tomato purée | 2 tablespoons double cream

Salt and freshly ground black pepper

A little chopped parsley, to garnish

To serve

Mashed potatoes and cooked peas

Bring the fish stock to the boil in a pan which will allow the pieces of cod to sit side by side in one layer. Add the fish, skin side up, bring back to a simmer and cook for 2 minutes, then turn off the heat. Ladle 800ml of the cooking liquid into a jug. Cover the pan of fish with a lid and set aside while you make the sauce. The fish will carry on gently cooking in the remaining liquid.

Melt the butter in another pan, add the flour and cook gently for 1 minute, stirring. Remove the pan from the heat and gradually stir in the cooking liquid. Bring back to the boil, stirring all the time, then leave to simmer for 10 minutes, stirring frequently, until smooth and thickened to a good sauce consistency. Whisk in the lemon juice, tomato purée, cream and some salt and pepper to taste.

Lift the pieces of cod on to a warmed serving platter and pull away the skin. Spoon over the sauce, sprinkle with chopped parsley, and serve with mashed potatoes and cooked peas.

Fish & Weed

This pattern really is steeped in Norfolk, but not Blakeney and Wiveton – instead it comes from time spent with Harry Cory Wright in his family's house westward along the coast in Burnham Market. Harry, along with his brother Charlie, is one of my oldest friends and he played an incredibly important role in the early years of the company: we mixed old habits of staying up late with the novel excitement of getting up early to take photographs in the first light. Harry is a compelling and original figure, something of a Tom Kitten with a plate camera; he combines old-fashioned elegiac steadiness with a mischievous twinkle. And he is a great model for the sartorial style of Old Town. (If you do not know about this remarkable company, I urge you to seek it out. Just one clue, they have a shop in Holt.) Harry's images of my early designs played a crucial part in establishing the Emma Bridgewater brand so swiftly and strongly. We put the pottery in unexpected places – on dusty stairs, in a tangle of dead rose branches, behind a broken window among rusty garden tools; we also captured the ware flying over the dunes, or submerged beneath the incoming tide – it was always a bit odd, but never dull or in line with contemporary expectations.

My favourite catalogue using Harry's pictures was produced in 1999, when we borrowed a small round tripod table from somewhere and drove it all over Norfolk, putting it up and covering it with ware in different landscapes, from piney Breckland to watery meadows along the Bure; we showed a tea party on the shingle beach at Salthouse, lunch in a rolling harvest field and children's pottery at sunset in the Broads. Whenever we worked together the days were invariably long and hard, but always punctuated with delicious snacks. From fish and chips in Hunstanton, via crab sandwiches from a window on the coast road, to pork pies in Aylsham, we were never in any danger of starvation, as we always bought, then photographed, then ate every single edible prop. Harry's energy and ingenuity provoked and inspired me along the way, and we always had non-stop fun (and often a tummy-ache).

The house belonging to Harry's family, a former shop in a street off the market place in Burnham Market, was at that time stimulatingly unsupervised; Harry's father was a very infrequent visitor, and his mother didn't stray out of Surrey any more, so the whole place bore the traces of years'-worth of boys' parties. This might have been a bit gruesome, but not a bit of it. Harry's father had a distinctive and graceful style, and in the 1950s and 60s he filled the house with elegant and particular furniture, pictures and china. His original scheme was now faded and battered, overlaid with piles of tapes and records, camera cases, fishing and sailing kit, and patinated by the passing years. Both brothers loved and looked after the place, but still, there were no grown-ups to call a halt to murder in the dark after supper ... Moreover, the house extended out behind, Tardis-like, dwindling into sheds and barns stuffed with never-to-be-restored antiques that were crumbling gently into ruins: all in all it was a paradise. And a prop warehouse of dreams.

When we were working on Brancaster beach, we used Harry's family beach hut as our base. The howling northerlies rolling in across the German Ocean in the winter months tend to play havoc with the dunes, sometimes re-arranging them dramatically so that we might have to dig our way to the door, then shovel out much sand before we could set our stuff out.

The china in Harry and Charlie's house provided one of my richest creative seams: I learnt a lot from the china on the kitchen dresser in Front Street. Not to mention the bathrooms. When I extended the collection beyond the first four shapes, I was aiming to fix and expand the mood of the brand as distinctively English, with a very close reflection of my style: I sought to use each piece to create a small surprise of pleasure – I had no sense of designing to build sales, instead I wanted to make a whole engaging picture. So rather than concentrating on new and different mugs (which would later on provide the commercial drive), I added a six-pint jug, a vase, a big soup tureen, and a large soap dish made in three parts. This soap dish has not been in production for years, but few things give me greater pleasure than unwrapping a new bar of Roger & Gallet soap and putting it into one of these big comfortable pieces. When I drew this shape I was thinking of the especially pleasing bathroom in Front Street. And the first pattern sponged on to the first sample was Fish & Weed. That soap dish also called for a washy version of chintz roses, being of an Edwardian sensibility. In all I wanted to conjure a cast-iron bath with a deep marble surround, a big old wooden bath rack, huge towels washed hard and thin over the years, cream lino, Jimmy Cliff on the record player next door, sun coming out – a fine Sunday morning.

The Fish & Weed pattern was for this soap dish. I just sat down and drew it, with all of this Norfolk stuff in my head, and I still love its simple playfulness. It has made a couple of reappearances over the years, but in writing about it I feel moved to have another look at it, and the results are shown here; they might pop up anywhere, so keep an eye out.

FISH PIE

This is an invaluable standby. You need frozen peas,
and I'd never put it on the table without tomato ketchup.

Serves 6

900g evenly sized, unpeeled, floury potatoes (Maris Piper or King Edwards)

175g cooked, peeled North Atlantic prawns

(those you peel yourself have a much better flavour and texture)

550ml creamy milk | 375ml double cream | 1 small onion, sliced

4 fresh bay leaves | $\frac{1}{2}$ teaspoon pink peppercorns

300g undyed smoked haddock | 300g cod or haddock fillet

200g salmon fillet | 115g butter | 3 large shallots, finely chopped

1 large garlic clove, crushed | 65g plain flour

3 tablespoons small capers, drained and rinsed

3 tablespoons chopped fresh dill | 50g Cheddar cheese, coarsely grated

Put the potatoes into a pan of cold water, bring to the boil and cook for 10 minutes. Drain well, then cover the pan with a clean tea towel and leave them to steam as they cool.

Squeeze any excess water from the prawns (you don't need to do this with those you peel yourself), lay them on some kitchen paper and leave them to drain.

Put the milk, cream, onion, bay leaves, pink peppercorns and fish into a large saucepan, bring to the boil and simmer for 8 minutes. Lift the fish on to a plate and strain the milky mixture into a jug. When the fish is cool enough to handle, break it into large flakes, discarding the skin and any bones.

Melt 65g of the butter in another pan, stir in the chopped shallots and garlic and season lightly. Cover and cook over a low heat for 10 minutes, until soft but not browned. Uncover, stir in the flour and cook gently for 1 minute. Remove from the heat and gradually stir in the hot milky mixture. Return to the heat and bring back to the boil, stirring all the time. Leave to simmer gently for 10 minutes. Season well with salt, then stir in the cooked flaked fish, peeled prawns, capers and chopped dill. Pour into a 2 litre ovenproof dish that is about 5cm deep.

For the rösti potato topping, melt the remaining butter. Peel the potatoes and coarsely grate them into a bowl. Fork through the melted butter and season well. Spoon the mixture over the top of the pie and sprinkle with the Cheddar cheese. Bake at 220°C/200°C Fan/Gas 7 for 35–40 minutes, until the topping is crisp and golden and the filling is bubbling hot.

Blue Shells

In the Outer Hebrides, in the 1970s, provisioning was quite as big a challenge as actually getting there. And the drive was an adventure. From London all the way to Uig in the north of Skye took around twelve hours if you did it in one go, leaving in the afternoon, with only a pit-stop at Tebay to eat a fry-up and fill the car and the petrol cans, after which you drove on through the night, there being a serious lack of places to stay en route; then, feeling spaced-out but a bit heroic, you arrived on the quay in the chilly dawn, where you might sleep uncomfortably in the car for an hour or so before the first Caledonian MacBrayne ferry to Lochmaddy. Crossing the Minch to the outer islands is almost invariably extremely sick-making and I had just one way of dealing with this: I ate chips, then dashed upstairs and, no matter how wet and windy, spent the two hours of the crossing on deck, longing miserably for dry land and trying unsuccessfully to lose myself in Georgette Heyer. From Lochmaddy to the house where we stayed was another drive, of forty minutes – so it took the best part of twenty-four hours to travel from smelly west London to the wild and magical Outer Hebrides.

> When playing with shell sponges to find different pleasing designs for plates, I was reminded of the folksy look of Sailors' Valentines – these are cardboard-backed stars and hearts crusted with garlands of shells around a seafaring scene under a small glass dome, one of the pretty things made by sailors as gifts for their sweethearts, to while away the long hours at sea.

The house where we stayed stands empty between family visits; its larder holds a brilliant store of dry goods, for which we might be bringing replenishments such as peanut butter or maple syrup, sea salt, black peppercorns or Provençal thyme; but short of bringing a carful of provisions (too dull!), you have to forage locally, then as now. There were basically just two shops (things have changed over the years, but it was still very simple in 1979): the solitary supermarket and the NAAFI in nearby Benbecula, which had arrived with the army. In these fine establishments we bought floury white baps, frozen mince, sausages, bacon, black pudding, salad cream and cheese – red or white? We rootled among the available vegetables, where the potatoes were plentiful and delicious, the cabbages OK and the carrots and turnips a bit limp: the rest just hopeless. Scurvy was always a possibility – never mind the dried herbs, it was *vital* to remember to bring lemons from London.

...nks.

cup (changing
downwards)

8 × Whelks
around

Small Tea Cup.

2" Plate

KEY { SCALLOP   STARFISH

WHELK   MUSSEL

COWRIE

} KEY

Small
Tea Saucer

11 scallop
Top row

10
Scallops
2nd row

11. Whelks
around
base.

10½" Plate
Starfish or

As shooting was the point and purpose of these trips, we were never short of delicious meat: we feasted on goose and duck. I don't think our studenty cookery skills were very good, but the days were very long and I remember being ravenously hungry. This is not surprising, as we got up before dawn to get out and into a place where you might get a shot at a duck or a goose; this operation was repeated in the afternoons, to be ready at dusk for the evening flight; during the day we roamed the bogs, swinging over the fences and trying to get close enough to those wary, elusive wild birds.

There was one other tempting source of exciting food: the sea. In those days there seemed to be no sign of a fish shop. When we met some men landing a boat on a beach we asked them about buying fish – any kind of fish – and they were very clear, none was for sale, as it was all pre-sold to a wholesaler who paid very good money. It turned out that while the home market was too mean at that time to buy fish enthusiastically, in Spain and Italy they were happy to pay handsomely for Scottish lobster, langoustines, prawns and scallops. The very thought of these scallops, landing just nearby and rumbling off to Madrid and Venice in refrigerated trucks, made us wildly determined to procure some. So we went on a mission; we realised that on a shooting trip we had passed the small factory where the scallops were processed, so we went back there and eventually persuaded them to sell us a boxful for cash. It seemed as if we had paid Savoy Grill prices, but it really was worth it. So the scallop shell is full of significance. It says delicious feasting to me; it has rarity value as food because it is hard work to harvest, and to underline this fact it is often sold as 'hand caught' because it is not possible to industrialise the getting of this fragile creature.

But the scallop has wider resonance: the beautiful shells are put to many artistic uses, such as shielding the modesty of mermaids, and providing a vessel for Venus as she rises from the waves in Botticelli's iconographic image of beauty; and then there is Maggie Hambling's so much larger than life, dramatic wind-blown scallop on the beach in Suffolk. And consider the grottoes and nymphaeums of classical antiquity which reappeared during the Renaissance as refreshing retreats. These curious architectural phenomena were brought home to Britain by young men who made the Grand Tour and thus saw examples such as the grotto in the Boboli Gardens at the Palazzo Pitti, at Pratolino, or the attractive bathing house (more suited to paddling and splashing, if you ask me) in the Palazzo del Te outside Padua. They were inspired to reproduce these effects, and grottoes were installed in villas great and small, becoming wildly fashionable in Britain in the eighteenth century. You can still admire examples at Clandon Park, Stowe and

Woburn. You can even experience one as your very own if you rent the Bath House from the Landmark Trust. Matthew and I stayed there several times, as it was just close enough to commute from when we exhibited at the Spring Fair in Birmingham: the cold plunge in the limestone pool beneath the shell-festooned bedsit is quite an invigorating thing for a February evening … The walls of grottoes are decorated principally with shells, and the inevitable swags and wheels led me straight to the pleasing idea of shells on plates.

And that's not all, for the scallop also has religious significance, being the badge of the pilgrim who has completed the Camino and walked all the way to Santiago de Compostela in north-western Spain. One of the legends of St James has it that he was beheaded in Jerusalem and his body sent home: the ship was lost in a storm off the coast of Galicia and afterwards the body was washed ashore, miraculously whole again, and encrusted with scallop shells. Many people make the pilgrimage on foot to Santiago de Compostela, and when we went there (by plane) I felt a strong envy for the dusty types arriving in the square with their well-worn boots and business-like staffs, with shells on their hats. This feeling was greatly intensified when we saw the drama of the huge swinging Botafumeiro, trailing clouds of incense, during Mass in the cathedral: it is not surprising to learn that during the spring and summer months the numbers of pilgrims goes up every year, for while we may have lost the habit of regular church-going, I believe that in the highly developed West we are still full of spiritual questioning, and the Camino seems to offer a deep answer.

So let's hear it for scallops, don't you agree? And while I love to add them to a fish pie for extra glamour, the very best way to eat them is that standby dish of the most traditional fish restaurants, utterly delicious Coquilles St Jacques. So here is a straight-down-the-line recipe.

COQUILLES ST JACQUES

Serves 4 as a main course (or 8 as a starter)

12 large cleaned scallops, in the shell | 50g butter
3 finely chopped shallots (50g) | 200ml dry white wine
600ml fresh fish stock, homemade if possible
25g plain flour | 4 tablespoons double cream
1 teaspoon lemon juice | 25g Gruyère cheese, finely grated

For the duchesse potatoes
800g peeled floury potatoes | 25g butter
2 large free-range egg yolks | Freshly grated nutmeg
Salt and freshly ground white pepper

Remove the scallops from their shells and cut each one horizontally in half, leaving the roe attached to one half scallop. Scrub 8 of the shells clean and dry them well.

Cut the potatoes into chunks and cook them in boiling salted water for 20 minutes, until tender. Drain well, then mash until very smooth. If you can press them through a potato ricer, that would be ideal. Stir in 25g of butter, the egg yolks, a little freshly grated nutmeg and some salt and white pepper to taste. Spoon the mash into a piping bag fitted with a 1cm star-shaped nozzle and pipe (or spoon) a border of potato around the edge of each shell.

Melt 25g of butter in a small pan, add the chopped shallots and a little seasoning and cook them gently for 4–5 minutes, until translucent but not browned. Add the white wine and simmer for a few minutes until it has almost disappeared. Add the fish stock, bring to the boil and cook until reduced by half.

Reduce the stock to a simmer, then add the scallop slices and the roes and cook them for 1 minute, until they are just firm and have turned opaque. Lift them out with a slotted spoon and leave to drain on a few sheets of kitchen paper. Then divide the scallop slices and roes equally between the 8 shells.

Preheat the grill to high. Melt the remaining 25g of butter in a small pan, stir in the flour and cook gently for 30 seconds. Remove the pan from the heat and gradually stir in the scallop cooking liquid. Return the pan to the heat and bring back to the boil, stirring. Stir in the double cream, lemon juice and some salt and pepper to taste.

Spoon the sauce over the scallops, sprinkle them with the grated cheese, then sit them side by side on a baking tray. Grill them for about 10 minutes, until bubbling hot and golden brown.

1

2

3

Prawns

I have a clear memory of cutting out this prawn motif. It was during the very very early days, while I was experimenting feverishly with all sorts of ideas for surface decoration; I had only just graduated to the foam cushions intended for cheap furniture, which offered an enticing surface on which to draw new, larger motifs for printing on the pottery, and I was working my way through the very first cushion. I wanted to create designs worth replicating, so they had to have a simple appeal, and had to work on the pottery shapes I had designed. I had just brought down my first batch of ware from Stoke-on-Trent, so I had a supply of biscuit-fired pieces comprising mugs, bowls, milk jugs and dishes and I was dreaming of ways to decorate each shape. Clearly prawns on mugs was not going to be a hugely popular idea, but on a dish, oh yes, I could see that. So I drew a rather clumsy prawn with googly eyes and mixed up a red colour, which I applied in a watery consistency to make the insubstantial pink of a cooked prawn.

Prawns, swirled swiftly in a hot frying pan with some oil, a knob of butter and two cloves of garlic (crushed but unpeeled, the better to remove them before serving them), was one of the dishes I most liked to make as a starter for the noisy dinner parties I gave at the time. My cooking is short on subtlety, I know it, and I have always stuck to simplicity, so as to minimise failures. These days I still love prawns, and I still cook them like this, with perhaps the addition of a chopped chilli or two, a spoonful of brown sugar and a squeeze of lime juice. And the first dish shape, just under thirty centimetres across, is the best thing to serve them in.

As I think this process through, I realise just how personal my pottery project was: the shapes were precisely intended for the life I was leading with my friends; and the patterns often have a direct explanation, a link to the detail of my culinary likes, habits and favourite things. From the beginning I understood that some designs would work across lots of different shapes, while others need only work on one piece. I can remember sampling prawns on the other three shapes, simply because I was pleased with the motif and wanted to use it, but it was only ever suitable for the dish. At the same time I was writing 'MILK' on the jug shape and stippling around the word with the fuzzy end of a real sponge for a marbled effect, to make my quintessential milk jug.

One of my godmothers gave me a copy of Caroline Blackwood's rather louche cookery book, *Darling, You Shouldn't Have Gone to So Much Trouble*, when it came out in about 1980, and I loved its cheekiness and adopted several recipes thrown carelessly down in it, such as Slapdash Goulash, Chicken

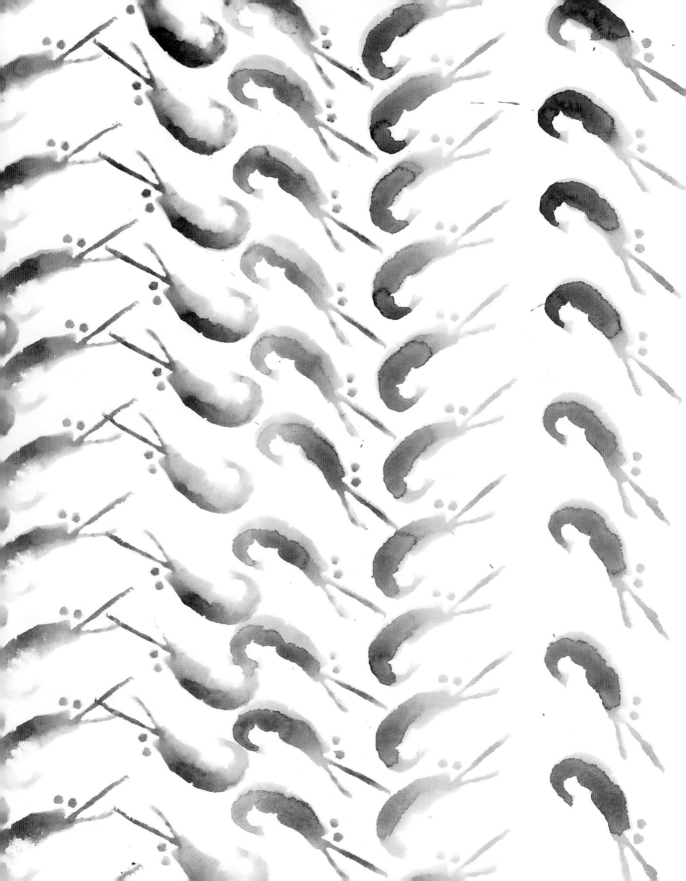

Soup (made entirely of combined tinned goods), Jonathan Miller's Saturday Salad and Thunder and Lightning – Henrietta Moraes's recipe for a pudding made only of cream and honeycomb. You get the picture, I think? The pleasure of cooking for a gang of friends I discovered while I was still at school; my cousin Kate and I gave as many dinner parties as our long-suffering mothers would allow. We had lots of friends in common in Oxford. Having next to no money, cheap ingredients were vital, especially as numbers were variable but on the ambitious side. So we were adept at spinning out spaghetti with tomato sauce. It's still a standby, but thank heavens the days of dried Parmesan dust (smelling slightly of sick, shaken out of a cardboard tub) are now no more. I completely take it for granted that I can buy a wedge of Parmesan cheese in the

Co-op in the village, but it's good to remember that it was not always the case.

We also favoured chicken in white sauce with rice, buying the very, very cheapest birds, whose life can only have been hellish, and padding out the chicken with lots of leeks, and even more rice. This too is one of those dishes that you can make on the cheap, as we did for our school friends, or you can make a heavenly version simply by using a top-quality free-range bird, poached with a few cardamom pods, and making a velouté sauce from the stock with the addition of a glass of vermouth. An alternative to fried prawns as a starter was often a mixture of cream cheese and mock caviar, with fingers of toast. And I remember often making a curious pudding that we were devoted to, which was a little individual hillock of tinned, puréed sweet chestnuts, rubbed through a sieve, with grated dark chocolate on top and a spoonful of whipped cream. This pudding is called Mont Blanc, and I was charmed to discover that it is the speciality of a Parisian café called Angelina on the Rue de Rivoli. A friend advised me to go there for a treat, and I discovered that the Angelina Mont Blanc is a stupendous event and suitable for at least two people and I think that a meringue was involved: my feeling is that the simpler version as described is a better bet.

> Oh how I miss my records! I loved the sleeve designs and I yearn for that scratchy sound, and I deeply resent having bought almost all of those vinyls all over again on CD ...

I can't remember more than this about the food I cooked as a student, for I am quite sure that I was more interested in who would be there, and what I was going to wear. In fact my most vivid pictures are of getting ready for those parties, and that may well have been by far the most fun part of them, because I always asked several of the girls to come early so that we could squeal and sigh together with Blondie or Elvis Costello playing loudly on a tinny record player as we shared bathwater, then borrowed and lent each other tights, shoes, eyeshadow – all in a haze of scent: Diorissimo, Chanel No. 5 for the sophisticated, Rive Gauche, and always the smoke from several Marlboro cigarettes.

Sometimes on a Friday evening a subterranean memory of that feeling of pure excitement resurfaces, and I wish very much that I was dressing up for one of those parties at which it seemed that anything might happen. But that particular thrill is all about youth, and the early days when you all start the race abreast with so much optimism and no idea of the pitfalls: you are immortal and the future is golden and boundless, or it will be if only he comes tonight – Tim, or David, or Guy, or whichever careless undergraduate it was that I loved that day ...

Sea Lavender

I am writing this in a café in the 11th in Paris. It's a beautiful September morning, and as I watch them, bright sunlight streams through the cigarette smoke of two men sitting outside, making a beautiful visual effect, sufficiently inspiring to sweep aside all health and safety nannying. I am sitting indoors, and not just so that the picturesque Frenchmen do not actually smoke all over me: I simply like being indoors, and sometimes I think that the prettier the weather the nicer it is to look at it through a window.

Which is perverse, because I dearly love to picnic. And while that might be under the willow in the field just beyond the garden, it is more likely to be a great deal more inconvenient. The most inconvenient, and by a long way the nicest picnic, sometimes known as A Picnic Too Far, is a breakfast picnic on the marshes at Morston, in Norfolk, on a morning in late summer when high tide is at around 8 a.m. For the best possible effect it should be a marsh tide, so that the creeks are brimming full, the moored boats in the Stiffkey river bobbing at the same level as the suaeda (seablite) bushes and the sea lavender. This is a long-standing event, which is repeated nearly every summer.

> We took a friend on a breakfast picnic at Morston and he was impressed but also slightly annoyed, saying it's so hard to unlock Norfolk's secrets that you really do need a native to demystify the marshes, whereas by comparison Cornwall is such a pushover, you more or less drive right on to most of the beaches. I knew what he meant, but kept my thoughts about St John's Well on the Camel to myself.

We would ideally leave the house with breakfast ingredients, barbecue, kettle and frying pan, plus swimming things, all marshalled at half past seven. Or something like. At least we do not any of us feel the need to arrive at the picnic under sail, but it's likely that others will, so the rendezvous is on. On a marsh tide you can't get far along the greens in the Land Rover, so there is quite a long trek, bearing burdens. When we get to the appointed spot, we will set up the barbecue and light it, then fortuitously the charcoal needs half an hour to heat to cooking temperature, so there is time for a swim. In late August the sea is pretty perfect for swimming, even the infamous North Sea. This morning swim is more bracing than the afternoon alternative (which involves walking all the way out to the harbour-mouth at low tide, then swimming home on the incoming tide over the sun-warmed sand), but it has the inestimable advantage of being followed by a slap-up full English. So we will wallow, and dive from the muddy banks, knowing the water is deep enough, and swim a few hundred yards out towards the harbour, then back, feeling the tide turn while we are in it, so that when we squelch up the muddy shore towards our fire, the boats around us are turning on their moorings. As the water recedes the children will certainly set up a mud-slide and get plastered with the delicious-smelling oozy brown stuff.

Meanwhile Matt and I will set to and make breakfast: coffee first, in an enamel coffee pot, then sausages and bacon, and toast made directly over the fire as it begins to cool, and last into the pan, fried eggs. I sometimes even manage to remember the home-made jam or marmalade, while Michael may well have smuggled a jar of Nutella into one of the baskets. If there is a sailing party, they will suddenly start dashing about to get their sails up again to get back around to Morston before the tide goes out too far and strands them, so there is a commotion. Then as they sail away, we can lie around on the rather muddy towels and feel full. If it's still sunny (I will admit that the weather is not always perfect, but it is often nicest early in the day), we might swim again before toiling home to pile the greasy pan and the picnic plates into the sink and leave them there for the day.

By late August the sea lavender is almost over – there are just a few last flowers casting the faintest, gauziest of purple hazes across the marsh, just a memory of the swathes of deep colour which shimmer across this beautiful shifting landscape through all of July. In the Marché des Enfants Rouges in the 3rd arrondissement in Paris I have seen bunches of cultivated sea lavender, sold as limonium, but the wild strain is my favourite by far, and I always pick a small bunch, mixed with the mysteriously scented artemisia which grows among the sea lavender, crab grass and occasional tufts of thrift, with bladder campion on the higher, drier spots. These wild plants dry out and maintain a whiff of marshy scent for months in a little jug on my dressing table, so there is always a sprig to hand, which was useful for the first sketches for Sea Lavender. This was a hand-painted pattern sold in the popular but short-lived range called Waterfield in 1989 and 1990. I developed this, and the other Waterfield designs, including Plums, Willow, Vetch, Ribbon and Bilberry, hand in hand with the paintresses, recruited chiefly for their good nature and careful attitude. Together we evolved flowing patterns based on repeatable brushstrokes to create a lyrical effect. Due to the success of other designs and techniques we have not recently revisited this experiment, but I love the handful of pieces that I still have at home.

HOUSE

I suppose it is all really down to Salvador Dalí, whose paintings I cannot love – the craze, the strong ongoing interest in unlikely decorative themes and motifs: I suspect it all goes back to putting lobsters in odd places and making teacups lined with fur. But I'll just put that on one side, as I looked at Dürer's engravings on another page during the lesson when my school art teacher Miss Hardy told us about the Surrealists. I don't think of it as exploring my unconscious mind when I take pleasure in unlikely juxtapositions; it seems more like a small private joke to see how silly a subject I can use to make a pleasing pattern with just a small jolt of surprise in it. When I made a pattern of a collection of vegetables in 1988 I added a potato because it seemed sufficiently unlikely. Similarly I love Bird & Worm (see page 97), because it's such a very lowly pair of creatures to repeat all over a teapot. And most of the patterns in this section have a dose of this idea of a little shock running through them: a tiny set of cutlery sprinkled all over mugs, plates and teapots; or an Aga and an ironing board as repeating decorative motifs – they are intended to make you smile.

But much as I like a far-fetched theme, I am also very focused on domestic life, so that I take much pleasure in decorating my pottery with homey images of intensely familiar things, from kettles and saucepans to pots of geraniums. I like to celebrate the everyday, the super-ordinary things with which we are so familiar that we almost stop seeing them. It's the same old same old – indeed there *is* nothing new under the sun – but as I consider ways to make patterns charming in an original way, sometimes it is by looking again at an object as familiar as a teaspoon or a vegetable paring knife that a gleam of inspiration twinkles out.

Aga Saga

While tidying up in the studio and embarking on the organisation of a fledgling design archive some years ago, we found a pile of big sheets of paper which had been sellotaped together to make huge expanses, the better to look at the repeats of a set of large-scale ideas, as I worked on them. These were some of the workings-out of the wave of designs for the collection of kitchen textiles that we launched in 1996. There was also an Aga Saga mug, available in brown, green and blue, in the previous year. These pages brought back so vividly the excitement I remember feeling as first I thought about screen-printing designs on to cotton to make into aprons, oven gloves,

tea towels, napkins and tablecloths, with some designs to be available as oilcloth as well.

I could not possibly have tackled this project alone, but Matthew turned to his mum for expert advice. Matt's mum is better known as veteran textile designer and queen of the National Trust tea towel Pat Albeck. She said that we *must* find and employ one of her former design assistants, a lovely girl called Jane Sweetser. We did as we were told, and Jane was brilliant. All the hard jobs were done by her; I watched her as she first put my Figs artwork into repeat and felt huge respect.

The collection contained patterns based on Figs, as mentioned, and Sweet Pea (Pat is responsible for the especially felicitous repeat in this pattern) and Olives designs, all already available on pottery; then, feeling inspired by the new vistas of a textile repeat, I felt that I wanted to break out and make patterns specifically suited to this new scale. So I thought about the important things in a kitchen, and I drew a set of my favourite kitchen implements – a pestle and mortar, a Sabatier vegetable knife, a copper pan, a palette knife and even an Emma Bridgewater salad bowl in LOVE pattern and a corkscrew. The resulting design was rather uncompromising but it is still one of my favourite patterns. In this case I worked out the repeat myself. But it was not destined to be a great commercial success; I think because the motifs, at life size, were pretty forceful. And all printed in a russet brown prosaically reflected in the pattern's name, Brown Kitchen.

Perhaps sensing that this design might be a bit special interest, or maybe just stimulated by its rather gigantic impact, this pattern inspired me to try something at the other end of the scale. The result was Aga Saga, where a different set of kitchen icons – this time consisting of kitchen table, chair, radio, ironing board and of course an Aga cooker, with a kettle, and a coffee pot – were all rendered at doll's house scale. At this time Joanna Trollope's masterly novels about domestic life as lived in old rectories, around Gloucestershire village greens and in Bath terraces were gaining terrific popularity, a huge readership and many imitators, which prompted some journalist or reviewer to coin a slightly acerbic collective term for this genre – the Aga saga. It pleased me to adopt this title, unironically, for I much admire her closely observed writing and I knew instinctively that many of my customers felt the same; moreover, lots of them confess to a deep love for their own Aga cookers.

What is it about these Swedish-designed ranges? They seem to draw devotion and contempt in equal measure. The devotion is probably most marked in people who, like me, grew up in fairly chilly houses, where rattly old windows and generally damp and draughty conditions combined with an aversion to spending money on central heating (gone, quite gone now or so it seems; as the globe warms we all seem happy to nudge the thermostat well north of eighteen degrees) created a real need for the constant heat source of the Aga in the kitchen. It was invaluable for huddling over to restart one's circulation after an hour spent essay writing. And the washing hung above it for economical drying in wet weather, while the dogs adored their spot under the table alongside the Aga, always cosy, and in the action, and to hand if needed to clean up Weetabix slops, flying toast crusts or, best of all, to tidy away the fatty and gristly bits when the meat is being prepared for a stew. It's also probably OK to generalise a little further about Aga-lovers: they know the value of a warming oven (four-oven model as opposed to two) for making perfect Melba toast, or for that matter the use of the roasting oven to make really toasty toast, than which there is *nothing* nicer to eat. Nothing in the whole culinary world. Most of all, Aga-lovers appreciate and make lots of two vital things: stews and baked potatoes.

And Agas look so friendly, with such an irresistible colour range to choose from – pale blue, navy, deep green, lovely simple cream or groovy lavender, all adding to the pleasure of that deep enamel, paired with gleaming chrome for the tops (or matching enamel in the older models, for real kudos); they are simply the best mix of form and function in cooking and they are deeply ingrained in our conscious pleasure in our kitchens.

Our house in Norfolk was just such a draughty fridge of an old rectory, as I have already mentioned: one day a lady turned up on a nostalgic visit, and it turned out that she was a previous inhabitant, one of many whom we met in our nine years there – so many that the house might almost have been a commune, but in fact it had functioned for years as two houses – and this lady had been the vicar's wife at the time in the 50s (yes, she was ancient, but that's the good thing about cold houses, they make you hardy) when the Aga was installed as a benefaction. She said that Lady Walpole's generosity had been practically life-saving, but that Aga apart, most of the house was simply too cold to use for six months of the year. We felt the same, and tended to huddle in the kitchen with an Aga at one end and a fire constantly alight at the other, eating variations on stew with baked potatoes followed by apple crumble, from October to March.

But what about the people who hate these friendly beasts? What kind of overheated, extravagant monsters can they be? Do they turn on their electric ovens like profligates just to bake some potatoes, or for that matter do they actually plug in their kettles? Ugh. Is their boot room heated for the dogs? Can they bear to eat toast out of a toaster? How? Don't they know what they

are missing? Well. They might be the sort of people who prefer constant reliable oven heat sources, maybe only sensing, or having swerved at, the horror stories of the Aga's entirely predictable Christmas sulking fit, which always means that at two on the big day the turkey is still raw, and by six, when it's finally cooked, the entire party are snoozing and hungover on the sofa. So they are a bit more orderly in their domestic planning, maybe; and they probably do more experimental cooking, following recipes involving chargrilling, fast boiling, deep-frying, perfect baking and in general the sort of precise temperature control only offered by a gas hob and a thermostatically controlled oven.

These Aga-refusers might also have done some building work recently, say a kitchen extension, or maybe a barn conversion. If this is the case, they are now so swaddled in insulation that they rarely turn on the heating at all, in fact just a few candles seem to make a room uncomfortably warm. The windows of that new build are ever open, and the heat detector had to be disabled the first time they cooked pancakes; frankly, if they had installed an Aga, and it was discussed early on in the project, they would have had to put the kitchen table outside in the garden.

Ah. I have turned into one of those people. It's all very complicated, and just a bit sad. The thing I miss most of all might only be the look of that old faithful, with its bumps and scratches, and its battered hot plates. And the Aga kettle. And I really can't bring myself to think about the toast ... So this pattern is a bit of a love song.

BEEF STEW

Serves 6

6 tablespoons dripping or sunflower oil | 200g bacon chopped into cubes
2 medium onions, halved and sliced | 2kg blade or chuck steak
75g seasoned plain flour | 4 fresh bay leaves
The leaves from 6 sprigs of fresh thyme
8 tablespoons mushroom ketchup or 4 tablespoons anchovy sauce
200ml leftover red wine | 1 litre fresh beef stock
Salt and freshly ground black pepper

Heat 2 tablespoons of dripping or sunflower oil in a large, reliably non-stick, flameproof casserole. Add the bacon lardons and fry until lightly golden. Add the onions and fry for 15 minutes, until they are soft and browned. Remove with a slotted spoon to a plate.

Cut the steak into 5cm pieces and toss with the seasoned flour. Add another 2 tablespoons of dripping or oil to the casserole and when hot, brown the beef in batches over a medium-high heat, adding a little more fat as and when you need it.

Return the onions and bacon to the casserole. Add bay leaves, thyme leaves, mushroom ketchup or anchovy sauce, red wine and beef stock. Bring back to the boil, stirring, cover with a sheet of foil and a tight-fitting lid and cook slowly at 150°C/130°C Fan /Gas 2 or in the slow oven of the Aga for $2-2\frac{1}{2}$ hours, until the meat is meltingly tender. Adjust the seasoning to taste, and serve with baked potatoes. (It is even more delicious the next day.)

Coffee Pots

Do you know that café on the Old Brompton Road in West London called the Troubadour? You may have heard of it, as it was a legendary venue for live folk music in the 1950s and 60s, doing duty for the whole of the equivalent scene in Greenwich Village in New York, where the Gaslight and the Kettle of Fish clubs, as well as countless marches and rallies, saw the launch of the careers of Joan Baez, Bob Dylan and others. The Troubadour was apparently Dylan's local when he came to London, and over the years many dazzling musicians have played there, including Paul Simon, Joni Mitchell, Linda Thompson, Elton John, Bert Jansch and Jimi Hendrix. Wow.

But actually I am marginally more interested in their marvellous collection of coffee pots. They fill the windows. They gripped my imagination from way back – I suppose I must have been driven past a few times, because they made me aware that I wished I liked coffee long before I actually did. I remember thinking about the distinctive differences between teapots and coffee pots, wondering why this was so, and how did it come about? But mostly I just loved them both. Coffee pots are slightly more foreign than the cosy, oh so English fat round teapot, don't you think?

Firstly, and most resonantly, they make me think of America, of the cawfee pot on the range in the settlers' cabin, or – better! – a battered red enamel pot, blackened in the embers of the cowboy's cooking fire; one trip to Texas was all it took for me to fall head over heels in love with this clichéd world of cowboys, bunkhouse cooking and campfires, a world so passionately evoked by Larry McMurtry and Cormac MacCarthy. In some moods, an enamel coffee pot can simply simmer with the dignified self-reliant spirit of a laconic west Texas sheriff who has seen it all, and still faces the harsh reality of life and the unforgiving landscape with his faith in God and his sense of humour intact. Other days, a coffee pot conjures a picture of an artist's garret in the Quartier Latin on the Left Bank in Paris, where a grubby, chipped – but elegant – porcelain pot warms on meagre heat from the stove while a skinny model shivers on a broken-down couch, and the painter scribbles on hungrily, oblivious to the delicious smells drifting up from the café on the street below.

Over the years I have collected quite a few English coffee pots – Carltonware, Denby, Poole, Myott, Palissy, Midwinter, Meakin, Johnsons and all the rest: the pleasure in these pieces, which are, to be honest, rather plain-Jane types, probably used for serving instant coffee, lies in their nostalgic air and unselfconscious jollity. They descend distantly but distinctly from formal silver and silver plate coffee services. It's hard to find grand old silver coffee pots in use these days, unless you dine frequently at high table in the fastnesses of the colleges of Oxford and Cambridge. We had a marvellous encounter with coffee pots one autumn half-term when I was not feeling energetic enough for the route march of our proposed holiday in Venice; we had an inspiration and instead booked into the Savoy, on the Strand in London. This was just a few weeks before that venerable old duchess of a grand hotel was subjected to an unflattering and unsuitable plastic surgery job. We were lucky to catch the last whiff of battered but sumptuous old-fashioned glamour; the children, to whom the staff were unfailingly sweet, thought that they were Eloise at the Plaza; and as well as the grandest of teas in the drawing-rooms

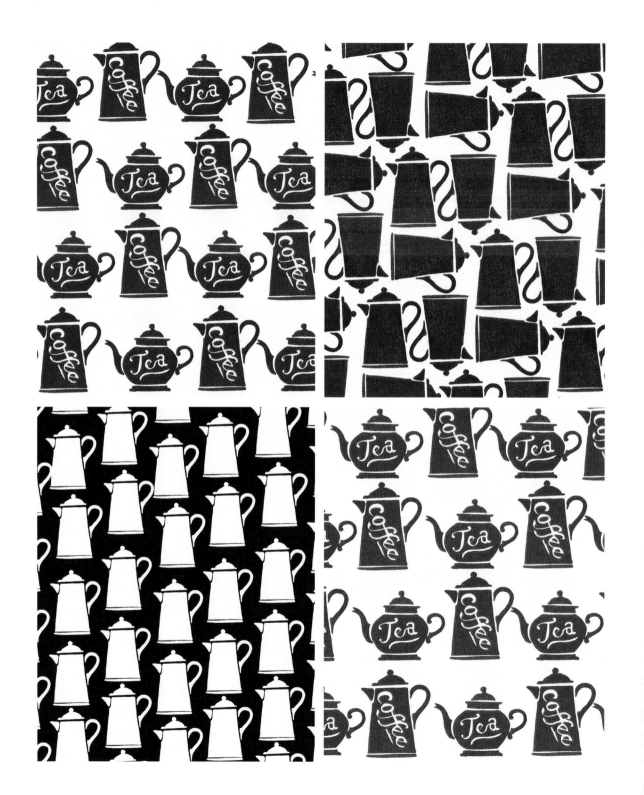

196

downstairs, we revelled in the room service. We had early morning tea in bed, then our delicious breakfast arrived on a trolley which metamorphosed into a dining table, which was set up in the window, with crisp snowy cloth and many shiny silver pots, for coffee, milk and hot water. Utter bliss.

Whilst driving across the Midwest from Chicago to Colorado Matthew became positively *desperate* for a cup of real coffee, no more burnt and watery cawfee for him (I had developed a perverse liking for the stuff). His need inspired him to study the road map and find, then urge me swiftly towards, the nearest town marked with the word 'Campus'. He rightly guessed that where there were students, there would be a real coffee shop. Panic over.

Granny's cousin Chloe, who is still upholding the highest culinary standards in her one hundredth year, has always made delicious coffee, and I try to emulate her, in this as in many other matters pertaining to civilisation. The coffee pot in her Chelsea kitchen was a brown porcelain one from Pillivuyt, with a spout at right angles to the handle – *very* French – and this had always to be warmed in advance. The coffee is, for first choice, beans, carefully selected and freshly ground immediately before use – and ground fine for filtering, because if you use coarse ground you will not get 'all the benefit', so you will wastefully use more beans to make less good coffee. A brown plastic filter, lined with an unbleached filter paper, is perched above the warm pot, then the ground coffee is tipped into the filter, and the kettle boiled. When it has boiled, take it off the heat and count to ten before you pour the water on to the grounds, so as to avoid the slightly bitter taste of boiled coffee; then refill the filter with water as it trickles into the pot below. Meanwhile swill the cups with hot water, and put some milk on to warm (never let it boil, as this makes it taste of school puddings!) I promise that this method quickly becomes second nature, and I love the rituals because they comfort me and distract me from eating too much toast. Mum always said that if you make the coffee really carefully (she too admired and followed all Chloe's methods), it's all the breakfast you want. Chloe adds one further step – she has a battered shallow tin bowl which lives beside the cooker for this one purpose only: it is half filled with water when the coffee is made, set on the lowest possible heat, and the coffee pot rests there, ensuring that the second cup is as good as the first.

In Honfleur last summer I bought a pale yellow Pillivuyt coffee pot, with its matching yellow (ceramic) filter: it is most satisfactory, but a bit fragile, as a result I believe of being kept warm on the stove over an asbestos mat. Chloe had this arrangement when I was young, but it was phased out when we all learned that asbestos was no longer the handy friend we had taken it for. (The builders discovered that our Oxford basement kitchen had been entirely damp-proofed with asbestos and we all suddenly had to wear gas masks to go in there until it was removed. A bit late, I thought ...)

The Coffee Pot design, from 1999, was only ever applied to a small straight-sided mug; it had an inevitable companion, Teapot, and they were both very pleasing. I especially like this mug, and managed to hang on to one for years; this is the final judgement on any pattern, as it is a huge challenge to hang on to my favourite pieces through house moves, not to mention half a dozen catalogue shoots at home every year, and a tendency for everyone to leave their mugs in cars, greenhouse, under beds and all over the garden.

With all this freight, and all these images – so widely varied, and swathed in customs, rules and snobberies – it seems to me that a coffee pot holds much more than just a stimulating brew to start us up in the mornings and keep us going when we flag. And this simply must be so when you look at any high street and count the large number of different coffee offers. So, what on earth *else* are we buying with our skinny mocha lattes, our grande americanos and our flat whites to stay or to go? Because it's more than just energy, of that I'm sure.

Here's the thing: I think we are buying a small piece of virtual real estate, a place to build a tiny daydream – which we clamber into to escape for a quarter of an hour from the mundane. Watch the solitary people in Costa: lots of them are clearly in a cabin somewhere out on their own landscape of dreams. And if they are not alone they too are staking a claim: they make a little friendship fort at their table, palisaded with flapjacks and muffins, safe from demands for the duration of a cappuccino.

Now don't be put off by the name of this cake, it might sound odd, but it's DELICIOUS. Mum was good at understanding how badly we needed something sugary to eat after school – so she often bought a bag of donuts, or iced buns (known to her as greased rats). Other days she made us this cake, and this one was popular along with Barbara Brunet's cake for Hungry Dragons.

BOILED BUNGALOW CAKE

Makes one 18cm square cake
450g good-quality mixed dried fruits
250ml water | 1 teaspoon bicarbonate of soda
225g caster sugar | 175g butter or margarine
2 large eggs, beaten | 100g self-raising flour, sifted
125g plain flour, sifted

Preheat the oven to 150°C/130°C Fan/Gas 2. Grease and line an 18cm square cake tin with non-stick baking paper.

Put the dried fruits, water, bicarbonate of soda, sugar and butter or margarine into a pan, bring to the boil, stirring, and boil gently for 15 minutes. Remove from the heat and leave to cool.

Beat in the eggs, self-raising flour and plain flour. Spoon the mixture into the prepared tin and bake for 1½ hours, or until a skewer, pushed into the centre of the cake, comes away clean. Leave the cake to cool in the tin for 5 minutes, then turn it out on to a wire rack and leave it to cool. Store in an airtight tin.

Knives & Forks

My china-shop revelation, that I would set up a company to make colourful kitchen crockery, took me to Stoke in search of a traditional British manufacturer who would be willing to make my ideas into a reality; some years earlier, in 1973, a vastly distinguished designer called David Mellor had founded his company with a parallel intention, in his case drawing on his knowledge of Sheffield, where he was born, to revitalise the making of British cutlery. His model factory, designed by Michael Hopkins and opened in 1990 at Hathersage, on the Derbyshire moors outside Sheffield, now managed by his son Corin Mellor, is well worth visiting: the building is beautiful, modern and purpose-built, it is garlanded with design awards and it sits alongside a delectable shop. There is also a David Mellor shop in London, which showcases his cutlery on Sloane Square: like many other couples, Matt and I had our wedding list there and still treasure many practical and lovely things from this great emporium of kitchenware, which has some of my favourite window displays. If you needed further incentive, there is also a small museum space at Hathersage where you will be amazed to discover what an impressive number of iconic and vital things have been designed by David Mellor beyond silverware for our embassies around the world, and steel cutlery for schools and hospitals. I will mention only traffic lights – you really should visit!

> The Jewellery Quarter in Birmingham strikes me as one of the most inspiring making places in England: all creative students, especially those studying jewellery, should visit some of the thrilling workshops and museums here.

David Mellor designs are simple and functional: beautiful and modern. They define a type of clean-lined, design-aware household. My parents-in-law, for example, still eat with the David Mellor cutlery they bought in the 70s and it suits them so well. My own personal preference is for older Sheffield wares, and in our kitchen you will find large flowerpots containing mismatched forks and spoons in silver plate of very varied quality, alongside knives with bone (or Bakelite imitating bone) handles somewhat the worse for their regular exposure in the washing-up machine. This type of cutlery, all British made, is easy to buy in antique shops and markets, and I'd rather replace the knives when their handles come adrift or the forks when their tines bend, than bother with the tyranny of hand-washing the cutlery separately. If I were to design my own range of silver, or silver plate cutlery,

I would have slightly outsize smooth fiddle-head shapes for the forks and spoons, and generous square section bone handles on the knives. I also love pistol handles on knives, mostly for their dashing name. Sadly it is very hard to envisage selling the vast numbers such a project would demand. So in the meantime we have had a jolly time putting colourful patterned handles on to foreign-made kitchen cutlery, but at the time of writing we don't sell any cutlery, except some dear little children's sets.

Spreading out some old newspapers and getting out the Silvo for a session of silver cleaning, perhaps before Christmas, or for a party, or just on a sunny weekday afternoon when you suddenly know it's time to ring the window cleaner because the sunshine demands some shining responses from indoors – this is one of those companionable chores which are so nice to share.

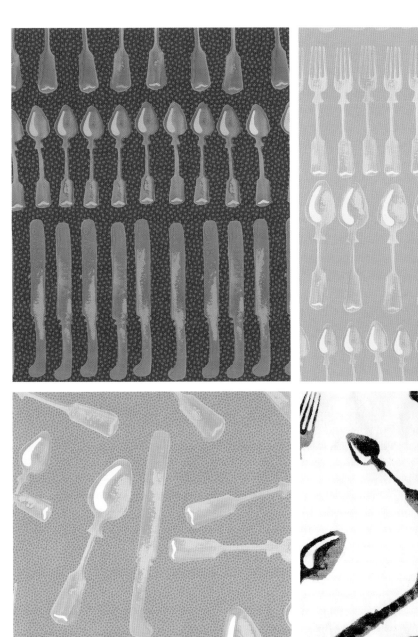
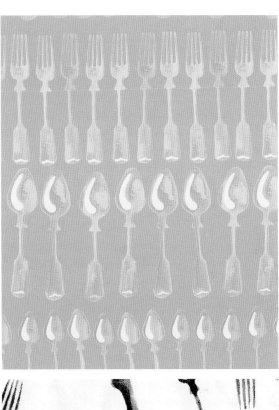
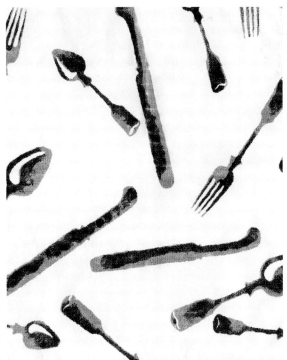

But if you do it on your own, well, you will have to turn on Radio 4 and hope for a decent afternoon play.

Sheffield is not only the home of beautiful cutlery; alongside table knives the city has specialist knife-making skills, so it is well worth investigating penknives, pocket knives and hunting knives for the Boy Scout types in your life. In fact I always have a knife in the glove compartment of my car, handy for an impromptu picnic – for slicing the salami, and opening the wine if you forget to buy screwtop – so Girl Guides too need knives. Don't be put off this subject by scaredy-cats, as a pocket knife does *not* define you as a strange and scary loner, though there's probably no need to carry one on the tube ... It is better that boys learn to handle a folding knife, along with a box of matches, nice and early instead of being forbidden them as dangerous.

We made some children's sets using Knives & Forks, but by far the best version of the design is the textile print we did, for which we used larger and much better-drawn artwork. The pattern was only printed in deep bluish purple, but despite this, it was all too easy to absent-mindedly think of the print as dropped cutlery, and I often found myself trying to pick a piece up as I cleared the table. This was because I drew the motifs in the silver I wished, in fact still wish, we owned.

You know that expression, 'selling the family silver'? It is not usually used in a positive context: you are not being kind about someone if you describe them as doing this. That is because it implies that the last of the capital is gone, and the assets are being cashed in ... But I often secretly think that it is what I am doing. My mum went out to work, a bit. But if she lived sensibly and frugally, something she was generally very good at, she could pretty much make ends meet without doing so. As she saw it, she had no need for a career (I speak of the period after her divorce from my father, and before Rick's career took off), because she had a small private income. Very modest, it was the tail end of the payout to her grandparents when their coal mines, along with many other privately owned heavy industries, were forcibly purchased by the Labour government after the Second World War. But when I left university, surprise surprise, there was no similar provision available; like the rest of the world I was going to have to make my own way.

It turns out, however, that I was blessed with a different form of capital: these assets consisted of a set of values, an insight into a wonderful way of living, and a big dose of energy. I set up my company in an overt and conscious attempt to conjure up some of the fundamental values and habits of my mother's and my father's families, to manifest these intangibles as lovely things, properly made and vested with the loving qualities of home: thus I think that it's as clear as can be that I too am busy selling the family silver. And that is no bad thing. I'm all for working with what comes to hand. And I see our old industries as rich seams for inspiration.

When I hold a large shiny soup spoon, I think of Maonie; she was a close friend of my Granny, and having had a glamorous career as a model she put this experience to work making beautiful dresses, including my aunt's lovely wedding dress. This dress survived the couple's departure from their wedding party on a bicycle with exploding rockets attached to it, and I last saw it on one of her sons at a fancy dress party ... But that's another story. Maonie always lived elegantly and austerely; she seemed only to own the very right things and nothing extra. The last time I saw her was at a lunch party, at which she served a delicious soup of brightest green, which we drank with large smooth silver spoons, whose bright and silky softness told you instantly that these were solid, not plate, and beautifully made and cared for. I cannot remember what the soup was made of on that sunny day, but here is a recipe guaranteed to be sharply *green*, and delicious on a summer day.

PEA GREEN SOUP

Serves 6–8

30g butter | 2 medium onions, finely chopped
2 large celery sticks, chopped | 1.5 litres vegetable stock
800g shelled peas | A large handful of watercress sprigs, plus extra to garnish
A pinch of caster sugar | Salt and freshly ground black pepper
2 tablespoons cream or crème fraîche (optional)

Melt the butter in a large pan, add the onions and celery, then cover and cook gently for 8–10 minutes until soft and translucent.

Add the vegetable stock, bring to the boil and add the shelled peas. Cover and simmer for 10 minutes, until the peas are soft.

Stir most of the watercress sprigs into the soup and blend with a stick-blender until smooth. Season to taste with the sugar and some salt and pepper, then stir in some cream or crème fraîche if you like a slightly creamier texture.

Coarsely chop the remaining watercress sprigs. Ladle the soup into a warmed soup tureen or large bowl, scatter over the chopped leaves and grind over a little more black pepper. Serve in warmed bowls, with a swirl of cream or crème fraîche if you wish.

Kitchen Utensils

I love patterns which reference favourite and familiar themes, so it's unsurprising that Matt and I have visited and revisited the panoply of kitchen equipment in search of decorative motifs. The original and first of several variations was a cookware range called Utensils in 1992 or 1993 for Ulster Ceramics, who also made our first oven to tableware, to a consistent good standard for about five years around this time. The design, Utensils, was a compendium of cookware, drawn as black silhouettes which formed a tightly tessellating border, with any gaps punctuated with eggs. I still use a couple of these pieces (proof of the good manufacturing achieved using government grant aid to Northern Ireland), but I'm afraid that sales were modest.

I made a much larger scale design using kitchen utensils, shown on a table here (page 213) this was for a collection of useful textiles in 1996 as described on page 189. This pattern, Brown Kitchen was shrunk down and sponged in pale grey onto a range of pottery for the Conran Shop in 2009. I like the drawing in this pattern particularly because every line is full of feeling and the choice of tools is personal and amounts to a homage of Matthew's cooking; it references all our favourite implements, things to cook, even actual places and events.

The tea towel hanging on the Aga rail in the picture opposite is a re-working of the designs for the Utensils kitchenware range made under licence by Ulster.

Matthew finds all machinery tiresome and loves the satisfaction of working by hand using really serviceable implements. So the Sabatier knife is his favourite piece. Which is not to say that his knives are well cared for, indeed not. I find them all over the garden, on window ledges in barns, even on the floor of the Land Rover (which has to be started with one). When they are all too maddeningly blunt he sharpens them on a doorstep; I prefer taking them to the butcher for pro treatment. Basically, he would always rather use a knife and a chopping board than a food processor. And I mostly agree, disliking uniformity and the ease with which a coarse and pleasing purée can become over-emulsified and gluey in a machine.

Brown Kitchen was modified to make another textile design the following year to incorporate some scattered vegetables and a colander. This is drawn from the one we have used since the early days of our marriage; it is enamel, slightly chipped, and larger than the pattern indicates (poetic licence!), which makes it a constant companion on trips to the garden. When I look at it I am reminded of the pleasure of composing the salad, on a day when rain has not recently splashed mud all over everything, when I can pick the very leaves and herbs that I want to make the exact salad I want to serve, with no washing needed. The sieve is the very one which lives beside the sink, where it is left for catching the tea leaves, which Margaret hates, as it means she always has to scrub it before she uses it for cake making.

There is one piece of kitchen kit from my childhood which I have often felt the need of, but dismally failed to resurrect, namely the Spong mincer which used to be screwed to the kitchen table whenever a shepherd's pie was to be made with the leftovers from the weekend's roast lamb. I bought one in the early years of our marriage, but somehow never managed to secure it satisfactorily. I compromise with hand chopping the cold lamb scraps then swiftly blitzing them in the Magimix, but it's not as I remember. Ah well ...

Thinking of cake making, I should have included a rolling pin, the one I use for pastry; pastry is something I believe that Matt will never ever cook, as he has an irrational nervousness about the dark arts of baking. I have seen him waving a rolling pin, but it was for violent purposes such as cracking nuts or bashing out an escalope – never the daintiness of preparing a flan case, or rolling out biscuit mixture for the children to cut out ... When I drew the corkscrew, I was in fact remembering the one from Mum's kitchen drawer – a true veteran. With no frills. Of course there has to be a pestle and mortar, truly the icon of our kitchen; I use it for grinding spices for curries and stews, also for crushing the Rich Tea biscuits for a chocolate biscuit cake, a ritual repeated for almost every family birthday – whereas for Matt it is a medieval (or do I mean prehistoric?) food processor, just perfect for making pesto with handfuls of fragrant basil from his greenhouse, pine nut kernels, grated Parmesan and best possible quality olive oil. Come to think of it, I'm going to try using it next time I make houmous – it might make a less sloppy result than the Magimix ...

And so it goes on – the egg whisk says omelettes (with cheese and a few chopped herbs, please!), and the palette knife (essential for flipping pancakes) is the one from a shop called Dehillerin in Paris. This magic cave of kitchen-ware is a last remnant of the days when this area of Paris thrummed with the vast food markets taking place every day. The address is Dehillerin, 18–20 Rue

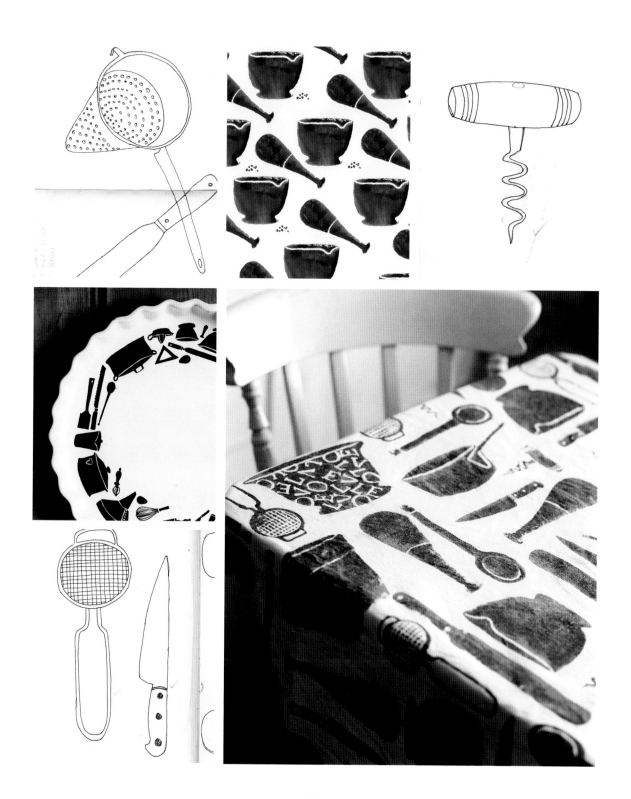

Coquillière, 75001 Paris, and you will never regret making the trip to find it, but as it is not possible (I assume!) to travel on the Eurostar with a suitcase full of deadly sharp knives, I ask the staff to pack up and dispatch my shopping to follow me home. If you too do this, I urge you to buy a cast-iron frying pan from this shop and have it added to the parcel; I still have the one that Mum bought there in my childhood, and once you have used this one, all other frying pans will drive you mad. But while it might get through security at the Gare du Nord, you will not enjoy carrying it down the length of the long continental platform – it weighs far too much!

When he was making a dark neglected room in the factory into a beckoning café, in around 2010, Matt used the sponges from Brown Kitchen in a more freeform way, sponging the utensils in dark red and at all angles on to a deep green background, knowing that this design would evoke our kitchen more clearly than any other decoration.

PRIMITIVE HOUMOUS

This recipe will form a rougher paste than you find in a supermarket plastic pot, and is lovely served with Nell's flatbread (see page 125).

Serves 3–4
1 x 400g tin of chickpeas | 1 tablespoon light tahini paste
Juice of 1 lemon | 200ml extra virgin olive oil
2 teaspoons chopped fresh mint | 2 teaspoons chopped fresh coriander
Salt and freshly ground black pepper

Drain the chickpeas and tip them into a large mortar. Crush them into a coarse paste, using the pestle. Add the tahini paste and lemon juice and mix together well. Then still working the mixture with the pestle, gradually drizzle in the oil, followed by a tablespoon or two of cold water, to make a slightly loose, coarse paste. Stir in the herbs and season to taste with salt and pepper.

Blue House

On our very first date, which started with lunch in Chelsea, Matt took me to the beach at West Wittering, where he had a beach hut. And after we swam we made sandcastles. Or, to be more precise, sand estates. I discovered then that Matt's head was full of plans for building and restoring houses, for laying out farms and gardens and playing with landscapes. It still is. And as with so many things, Matt has developed his ideas much more fully and intricately than other people seem to. Or more than me, anyway. This is the difference – my brother Tom and I played farms, happily, even devotedly as children; actually I mostly hogged it, encouraging him to set up a garage on the road alongside so that he didn't interfere with my layout of the hunt coming through the farmyard. Anyway, we were very absorbed in our arrangements, and we didn't hesitate to draw the road plan on to the playroom table with thick felt pens (Mum really lost it when she found this out), though a few hours later we jumbled it all back into its boxes, mixing three-legged lead cows with plastic sheep and a miscellany of makeshift tin and plastic fencing and walls. It was all hit and miss, with disabled stock in unlikely mixed herds and leaning on trees, fences and each other to stay upright. And we soon abandoned the farm in favour of a fight on space-hoppers, or building a tree house in an apple tree with a saucepan rack on a length of string as a retractable ladder to stop Sophy getting in. Meanwhile, at the same time, in Chiswick, Matt was taking his farm a great deal more to heart; he and his father made regular trips to Bonhams and the Portobello Road, for toy sales to complete his lead farm, down to the very last village idiot and milkmaid – not one character, animal or piece of kit is missing. And he (still) likes to lay it all out and keep it on the window seat as a (beautiful! factually correct!) installation, and for several days he will tinker carefully with it. From the beginning he was committed to farms, where we were just playing.

The Blue House design, dating from 1990, is one of Matt's first forays into design for Emma Bridgewater, and it strikes me now as quietly but tremendously significant, pointing as it does to his keen real-life longing, expressed in sand at low tide at West Wittering, to achieve not just a house, but a whole developed, thought-out landscape. The pattern is rare, both because we were still a tiny company at that time, and also because we did not make many pieces in Blue House, so any survivors are fairly unusual. The appealing classical house was enlarged, with pavilions, lodges and avenues, when decorating big meat plates and dishes, while on smaller pieces such as mugs the house stood alone, with deer among trees in the distance.

This spongeware design works for me because, whether with serious intent, or as just one of many joyful childish games, we all like playing house, don't we? This is why so many toys, from Fuzzy Felt farms (definitely a strong underlying influence for me; I *loved* Fuzzy Felt) to doll's houses, and even those dear little Swedish bentwood boxes containing small houses, trees, people and animals – they all appeal to a childish desire to order and boss a tiny world.

Matt has remained faithful all his life to his admiration for a well-ordered, farming-orientated home in the country; meanwhile I have much more mixed-up desires – I love planting apple trees, and buying salad seeds for the polytunnel and all that, but now the children are nearly all grown up I realise that I am happy in a city for at least part of the year, where there is no need to put on gumboots to put out the rubbish, no kindling to split, and a friendly café and an art house cinema close at hand. Best of all, there is no need to get into a car from one week to the next. So I am not quite Johnny Town Mouse to his Timmy Willie, but nearly.

Over the years we have done numerous special designs, for museums, schools, department stores and cathedrals as well as for events such as Royal weddings and the Chelsea Flower Show. These designs are pretty well without exception applied to mugs, and my favourites are the series that Matthew designed for the Churches Conservation Trust, as they are rich in architectural detail.

Matt's Blue House pattern grew, soon afterwards, into its natural, real and true manifestation when we were asked to make a huge hand-painted bespoke dinner service for a big house in the Scottish Borders. This happened soon after we found ourselves, slightly shell-shocked, as the new owners of Sam's small factory, when it was hard not to feel overwhelmed by what we had just done and wonder feverishly why on earth we had hobbled ourselves with our own manufacturing. Painting a dinner service of several hundred pieces had no bearing on the business, as we had no plans to develop a bespoke offering. I was always completely clear that Emma Bridgewater was about scaled-up making: I wanted to reach out to as many kitchens as I could. But there was a real comfort and reassurance in the challenge of making one knockout, amazing thing in the factory that was now ours: if we could pull it off, it justified the crazy fact of us owning a pottery. Illogical, but there it is.

So Matt went to the Borders, spent a few days on the estate in question, and painted about twenty lovely watercolours of the house, its landscape and some picturesque details. Then in conversation with the client he refined these paintings into a series of twelve images which were to be reproduced across the dinner service. There followed a confab with the butler about shapes and numbers as well as practicalities such as durability and future replacements. It was all carefully worked out, and we went through great anxieties about our ware: would it actually be *good* enough for such a grand project? I had never had any doubt that cream earthenware can be as refined as bone china and porcelain, which is what most people turn to when considering a dinner service for best. Just think of Wedgwood's Napoleon Ivy, but wasn't Sam's making, that we had just bought, rather, well, clunky? We did making experiments, and found that it was possible, particularly as the results would in this case always be washed up by hand, to cast the jugs, cups, teapots and all hollow-ware much lighter than usual. We have a handful of pieces which were rejected and replaced, and I marvel at them when I pick them up – the plates are almost as light as poppadoms, the coffee cans (made especially for the project) like blown eggs, they are so fine.

With Derrick Lloyd, our truly wonderful head decorator, Matt evolved a formal border which was to be painted on to every single piece of the service, incorporating stylised leaves and very fine banding. Several versions were proffered for inspection, from which the client chose his favourite. Then Matt recruited a team of painters capable of helping him in his task of reproducing the twelve watercolours across the service. Each piece of serving ware was to bear a landscape and a border, while some pieces such as dinner plates and saucers would only carry the border. The task force included his father and an old friend called Jane Langlands, but Matt did the lion's share. Once each landscape was complete and satisfactory, Derrick added the border, then followed the trauma of firing, which inevitably caused a significant proportion of losses, necessitating the complete replacement of each lost piece. It was a stressful and tiring project – Matt confessed afterwards that it was one of the hardest things he has ever done. But the result was triumphant, extraordinary: everyone in the company had been involved at some point, and we felt proud, and finally, much less daunted by our factory when we despatched the finished, carefully wrapped, masterwork.

Blue House

LETTERING

There is a long and not especially honourable tradition of writing on pottery. Before glass was produced cheaply, earthenware was what most people drank their beer and cider out of when they went to a public house, and pub humour, as exemplified by the sort of plaques still often displayed behind the bar, bearing messages such as 'You don't have to be mad to work here, but if you are it helps' was echoed on early drinking wares which made visual puns such as the pottery frog at the bottom of a tankard of cloudy cider, or the trick mugs which poured your beer in your face, alongside patriotic and political slogans such as 'Wilkes and Liberty' or 'Reform' (referring to the great Reform Bill of 1832). Moreover in domestic life, for example, in a busy kitchen, labels identifying the contents of otherwise identical vessels would be of obvious use, so Milk, Cream, Gruel or whatever are written on utilitarian creamware for ease of use.

As with so many other ideas, actual innovation and real novelty are extremely unusual. Instead, when decorating, all craftsmen and designers spend their working lives revisiting, re-imagining and recycling old themes. We hunt high and low for new ideas, hoping all the time to strike a new seam. Lettering, print and typography – especially if it's old and odd – these all hold a fascination for Matthew, who says that he has been fiddling around with typefaces and polishing up his handwriting since his first days at Bedales, where his friend Edward challenged him to be precise: was he reproducing a legal or a clerical hand? Was it mid or late eighteenth century ...? All pure Greek to me. But I share his enthusiasm for punchy type once we are talking about interesting themes, such as agricultural sale posters, which he collected and wallpaper-pasted to the walls of a small hall at home; or the Nashville equivalent as morphed into provision of posters for performances at the Grand Ole Opry. Hatch Show Print is a strange survivor from the late nineteenth century, its barn-like premises on Main Street in the country music capital of the world a thrilling find on an American road trip. We brought home many posters, and even had our sale poster printed there one year as well as two party invitations, just for the sheer wanton thrill of being a customer of such an unlikely business. They have never thrown anything out, and the blocks carved for farm sales in the 1900s are still in use, jumbled with lettering from the 50s and 60s for Elvis, Patsy, Johnny Cash, Waylon and all those huge stars. Total pleasure. And totally inspiring.

Equally Matt is thrilled by old-fashioned sign writing – we have some around the factory; and he is passionate about passing on his lettering skills, to make sure that we can hand-write posters and menus and hold back in a tiny way the dreary homogenisation of local poster-making on computers

– almost always disastrously dull and inelegant. So it's not surprising that even before we hit on the Toast range we had already experimented with Milk jugs, mugs emblazoned A Present for a Good Girl, in imitation of nineteenth-century Sunday school prizes, alongside personalised mugs, at first for our children, wider family and friends and soon as part of our range.

As is plain to see, my own unaided attempts before I met Matt are very limited, if enthusiastic; his graphic expertise and enthusiasm is a fundamental strength within the company.

Toast & Marmalade

This range – now embracing a vast number of themes and colours across a wide array of nice things, including tea towels, tablecloths, hand creams and toiletries, shopping bags, cutlery, stationery, tins, melamine picnic ware and more – is still first and foremost a range of pottery. Colours will come and go, but I sense that the writing, in plain, uncompromising black, will always be the very best of it. Certainly I always have the first five pieces in my mind whenever we set out to do something new with this simple, powerful pattern: that is, a half-pint mug, a side plate, a French bowl, a teapot and a milk jug. Of these pieces, the mug and the teapot have since been revisited and redesigned, but the others are unchanged. The evolution of these five items defines the very heart of the company, the best example of how Matt and I work together, as well as being the truest explanation of why we ever make anything worthwhile. Toast came about painfully but swiftly; we collaborated efficiently, drawing on each other's core strengths and achieving an end result which holds not a trace of compromise: just occasionally you know that you did something really well, and this is it for me. And I only write the copy.

The little plate marked simply 'PLATE', opposite, is from the Utility range produced in 1998, and the one on the bottom of the pile is from the set that we decorated for our very first house when we got married.

I have described elsewhere the jolt of pure recognition I felt, some time in the early 90s, when, during one of several purgatorial stints at the New York Gift Fair, Mrs Mottahedeh gave me a facsimile of a plate designed by Sylvia Pankhurst bearing the slogan 'Votes for Women'. What I know is that it acted like developing fluid on my imagination, reacting with a childhood attachment I had always felt for Mum's creamware jug bearing the word GRUEL. I instinctively understood that between these two items a big secret, a powerful thing, lay just beneath the surface; I needed only to bring it out into the light. In the basement office in Fulham, Matt and I sat down to tackle this excavation, and as I admit, it was painful. We always clash, sometimes loudly, when tackling a new design – it seems to be an almost violent process involved in breaking through to newness. But whereas a new design often takes us a long, agonising time, sometimes producing a subtly compromised result, this time we cantered through various ways of combining lettering with pattern, disagreed rudely as usual, but didn't dig into opposed positions, instead working

693
Fulham Rd

PLATE

The KITCHEN ★ PLAY ELVIS & DANCE AROUND

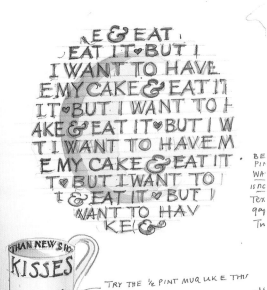

THAN NEW SHO
KISSES

TRY THE ½ PINT MUG LIKE THIS

scale

BE
PIN
WA
is no
Tex
9ay
Tu

I LOVE YOU MORE THAN

on through, and within maybe as little as a couple of hours we had dispensed with the decoration to focus on classic black capitals, expressing our simplest, most heartfelt pleasures when it comes to food.

The plate came first; now this plate, measuring $8\frac{1}{2}$ inches, is strictly speaking a side plate, but for me it has always been my favourite piece, the thing I use most often, on which a good pattern looks its very best. From the first day of the company I have taken a subjective line, asking myself *all* the time if I am making a personally honest decision – about finance, people, design, everything – and somehow this range is often a prime opportunity to fly a very personal flag.

> Driving through France as a child I loved the faded Pernod advertisements painted onto barn walls, and have felt sad as they faded clean away. So I am extremely happy to note that as the digital world whirls ever faster, we have once again taken to sending men up ladders to spend all day writing beautiful signs.

Matt drew round a plate and started to doodle with lettering styles while I fretted about how to say the very truest thing that I could on a plate. Because Sylvia Pankhurst's heartfelt cry could not be betrayed with a flip joke. Am I exaggerating? On the whole I think not. Matt announced that if we wanted to write in capitals that sat comfortably, filling the rim of the plate, I had to use around twenty-five characters. He experimented knowledgeably with small significant lettering variations, veering always towards strength and simplicity, while I came up with the legend TOAST & MARMITE, KEDGEREE. Because if I had to Desert Island choose what one thing I could have on toast, it would be Marmite, and so the first batch of print said MARMITE. But one of the team suddenly saw this, rather late in the day, as we had already printed a batch of litho to decorate the very first plates. We swung into action, agreeing that it was not acceptable to put someone else's brand name at the heart of what was, even from the first day of the first show at which we made the range available, going to be a big deal pattern for us. With a little bit of jiggling we substituted MARMALADE – also a vital ingredient in a happy kitchen. So I need to say that if you bought this pattern early on and you have a plate which says TOAST & MARMITE, it is truly rare, as we put the brakes on very quickly and only a tiny number of these were ever made. Perhaps no more than 150. And I only happen to have a couple because a man blustered into the Fulham shop one day demanding replacements for some Toast plates on which the glaze had crazed. He fibbed and insisted that the plates were no more than a year old, and he was so vexed that Jamie thought it better not to argue the point, though he could see from the profile of the plate (they were very fine and light in the early years) that this was most definitely not the case. He didn't notice the different wording, and the plates sat on a shelf in a back room: I only spotted the telling word MARMITE quite by chance ...

The range was, as we knew it would be – it was obvious from the first samples – a big success. However, as I write this I do recall having to offer it to Liberty on a sale or return basis at first, which we hated to do, and usually avoided. But from 1994 onwards we added to Black Toast, and the wording across the range of shapes is a defining vocabulary, where bubble and squeak, quinces, lapsang souchong, chicken pie, pea soup, treacle steamed pudding and custard described our customers to themselves in a way that the many imitators of this idea have struggled to understand or re-create.

In 1998 we re-created the range in cobalt blue, and then in 1999 in Cambridge blue without changing the wording. In 2004, with prodding from a newly convened commercial team, we rethought this decision and made a fresh, more compelling blue range with different wording. Before that I had a breakthrough and wrote I LOVE YOU MORE THAN CHOCOLATE in pink, on a cup and saucer: this proved very popular. There was also a health-conscious version, ORGANIC & GREEN. This was not as strong as the others, I think maybe because our customers are typically too sensible to focus overly on this issue; my feeling has always been that Emma Bridgewater customers are frequently people who cook from scratch and swerve around faddiness. And since that first venture into lettering we have experimented continuously and always pleasurably, in search of felicitous combinations of words and ideas in all sorts of colours.

Once the cat was out of the bag, and we knew how powerfully people respond to simple messages, we started to play a little, and I very much enjoy the jokey tone that has evolved. Some of my favourite pieces in the range are light-hearted (though still heartfelt!) and they include BIG LOVE, and I LOVE YOU MORE THAN ELVIS, both on pint mugs, LAST NIGHT I HAD A VERY NICE DREAM ABOUT DANIEL CRAIG on a tea towel, LOVE & KISSES on a teacup, MADE IN STOKE JUST LIKE ROBBIE WILLIAMS in red and blue on a half-pint mug, and PEACHES IN THE SUMMERTIME, as well as TRUE LOVE & HIGH ADVENTURE, also on mugs, both in pillar box red.

I can't finish without giving you a recipe for a delicious kedgeree.

KEDGEREE

Serves 6

50g butter | 1 small onion, finely chopped

The seeds from 6 green cardamom pods | $\frac{1}{2}$ teaspoon ground turmeric

$\frac{1}{4}$ teaspoon mild curry powder | 5cm piece of cinnamon stick

1 teaspoon harissa paste | 4 fresh bay leaves | 350g basmati rice

600ml hot chicken stock (ideally home-made)

Salt and freshly ground black pepper | 350g undyed smoked cod fillet

350g undyed smoked haddock fillet

3–4 medium free-range eggs (optional)

3–4 tablespoons double cream or crème fraîche

3 tablespoons chopped curly-leaf parsley, reserving a little

for garnish if you like

1 tablespoon freshly squeezed lemon juice

Melt 25g of the butter in a large saucepan, then add the onion and cook gently over a medium heat for 5 minutes, until soft but not browned. Add the cardamom seeds, turmeric, curry powder, cinnamon stick, harissa paste and bay leaves and cook for 1 minute. Add the rice and stir until it is all well coated in the spicy butter. Add the hot chicken stock and $\frac{1}{4}$ teaspoon of salt, bring to the boil, then stir once to release any rice from the bottom of the pan. Cover with a close-fitting lid, reduce the heat to low and leave to cook very gently for 12 minutes.

Meanwhile, lower the smoked cod and smoked haddock into a pan of simmering water, bring back to the boil and cook gently for 4 minutes, until just cooked through. Lift on to a plate, and when cool enough to handle, break the fish into large flakes, discarding the skin and any bones.

If you wish to serve this with eggs, hard-boil them for 8 minutes. Drain, cover with cold water, then peel and coarsely chop.

Melt the remaining butter. Uncover the rice and remove the bay leaves and cinnamon stick. Fork through the smoked fish, the chopped hard-boiled eggs if using, and the cream or crème fraîche. Cover again and return to the heat for a couple of minutes, until the fish has heated through.

Gently stir in the chopped parsley, melted butter and lemon juice and season with a little more salt and black pepper to taste. Serve sprinkled with a little more chopped parsley if you wish.

&CREAM·PROFITEROLES&

TEA&COFF[EE]

SPRINKLE&

SWEET PEAS
ZINNIAS·PEO[NIES]
&CORNFLOW[ERS]
·ASTERS&

NICE STRONG COFFEE·

WHIP·SIEVE&SCRAMBLE

FOLD·MIX·STIR

POUR&COMBINE

SAGE&MINT
BAY LEAVES
DILL&SUMMER
SAVORY·BASIL
CHIVES&FLAT
LEAF PARSLEY
MARJORAM

APPLE
CRUMBLE

PASTA·SORREL
RISOTTO&
SOUP·

IRIS·SANDAL[WOOD]
&JASMINE&L[IME]
JASMINE&LIME·S
·LIME·S

PARTIES & FEASTS

SHAKE IT
SHAKE IT
SHAKE IT

TOSS

WHISK
CREAM
BEAT&
MASH
NICE
FLOWERS

GINGERBREAD·VICTORIA SPONGE & CHOCOLATE CAKE·

FINGERS·BOILED EGG & TOAST

ES·
S
HLIAS

D&VETIVER·ROSE·GERA...STEPHAN...LIONOTIS·J...

HOT CHOCOLATE

BACON & EGG·BUBBLE & SQUEAK·

KEDGEREE·TOAST & MARMALADE·

FESTIVITIES·FRIEND...FAMILY &

2 PINTS·A QUART
THAT'S ¼ of a GALLON

COFFEE·COFFEE·COFFEE·COFFEE·

A Present for a Good Girl
& a Good Boy

People often ask, which pottery companies do you regard as your main competition? And the answer is simple, none of them. I am completely clear that we are successful for one reason only, which is that people are sweet – they love to give each other presents. And if we can make our wares so tempting that when they buy a present for their best friend, afterwards they come back to buy another, for themselves, then that is the signal that a design is working. We are in the gift business, it's that simple. When Christmas shopping I know that I might well dither between a book, a CD, a scarf and a mug, for example, to give to a friend: so we are focused on making lovely things, things you need, and things that inspire, tempt or amuse – or, best of all, all five at once.

There used to be a legendary antique shop on Stamford Bridge in Fulham: the name on the battered fascia was Stephen Long, and the man himself was often seated at a table in the gloom at the back of the shop, while his window was always full of delectable china and glass, all most temptingly arranged. Stephen had a special feeling for little mugs with names, mottoes, messages and dear little engraved designs showing children playing, and from him I learned that these were often made to be given away as treats and prizes at Sunday school: my favourites were the ones bearing the legend 'A Present for a Good Girl (or Boy)'. I often visited, and leaving my bike outside I would yearn through the stock, unable to afford, in those very early days of the business, any but the most chipped and damaged things. So it was a short step from loving these endearing mugs to creating my own version of them. It was with Stephen Long's children's china in mind that I drew a small version of the half-pint mug shape; it was to be a little squarer, dumpier, but still with a foot that seemed to have been turned on a lathe, and I called it the Baby Mug; we are still making this shape today, as it is indeed nice for children, but it is also very useful for a little cup of coffee, or a tisane in the evening. I also drew a flat bowl, useful for nursery tea, known as the Baby Bowl, and my Good Girl and Good Boy patterns were usually made available on all three of these shapes.

The lettering was cut out in one sponge, and it was exciting to realise just how versatile hand printing on pottery could be. In the nineteenth-century versions, the children are rewarded for their goodness with hoops, tops, pigeons, canaries in cages, kittens and bows and arrows: in its first incarnation as part of the Emma Bridgewater range in 1985, I illustrated the Girl mug with a basket of flowers, while the Boy had a boat, and over the following years I did several versions, substituting teddies, kites, train sets, Noah's arks, cupcakes,

a roundabout and some nice old-fashioned toys such as tops and marbles. My very favourite ones were in 1998, when the Boy was rewarded with camping kit including a tent, a frying pan and a string of sausages, while the Girl pattern was of a dear little fur-trimmed outfit with matching boots and hat. I am told that these designs were often bought for grown-ups, and as we have not carried these little gifts for ages, I think that it is time to revisit the genre. As is so often the case, old china provides invaluable clues and inspiration, offering so many ideas which are well suited to reappraisal and realising anew.

For a fashionable 1980s shop called Eximious I did a pink-printed version of the pattern A Present for a Good Girl (1986). This early venture into printed decoration was, as Sam, who was still making for me at the time, predicted, not financially successful, despite selling several hundred pieces, as the minimum print run left me with a large, reproachful, expensive pile of obsolete print for mugs which would never be wanted. This was my first mini version of the potentially lethal crisis that is stock management (or mismanagement): costly unwanted print was one of many huge adaptation challenges afflicting the industry at the time. I understood intuitively when I set out that life and tastes were changing, that with more women joining the workforce every day there was a sharp decline in domestic formality; couples stopped wanting to acquire a whole matching dinner service when they set up home – not least because by the time they married they had probably been living together for some time already, and they had bought many of their household goods for themselves. But although the writing was on the wall, many of the factories looked the other way and hoped for a return to the old ways. The whole industry was hung up on a promise, a promise that if you bought Old Chelsea, Willow pattern, Napoleon Ivy, Blue Italian, Beryl, Royal Albert, Dresden Sprays, Homemaker and all the rest of the marvellously evocative dinner services you would be able to buy replacements and additions for ever. I visited factories stacked to the rooftops with outdated wares, teapots without lids, saucers with no cups, and both in shapes and patterns that nobody would ever need or want again. And they had further embarrassment in the form of rooms full of the print for those missing lids and cups and all the rest, all equally undesirable, all counted annually – I feared, gloomy as Eeyore – and given value on doomed balance sheets. It was a whole great beached-whale of an enterprise. Sadder still, the demise of one company was very likely to pull several others under, as the industry was very intertwined with countless, sometimes fatal, mutual supply arrangements.

> Some of the old businesses in Stoke-on-Trent – those that didn't disappear in the 70s and 80s – went to look for production abroad in developing countries with low labour costs, a story we all know. BUT I truly believe that in the future some of our heavy industries will once again flourish in the Midlands, with zippy up-to-date management, attitudes and controls.

So my plan to provide resolutely informal pottery shapes, and encouraging my customers to mix designs freely, was doubly fortunate and timely because I was, rash escapades notwithstanding, dedicated to hand printing, which eliminated that tell-tale unsold, unloved print pile-up.

And fortunate is the word – I knew none of this when I set out, and I definitely landed on a tight formula by good luck, coupled with no cash!

This venture was a stern lesson which gave me an aversion to print, especially coloured print – *so* pricey – which I clung to for years. It was 2002 before we did a children's coloured range, inspired by the success of the first Birds in 2000. For children we did a Chick, a Duckling and a Bunny and these proved immensely popular. Perhaps this was not surprising, as until 2002, following on from Good Girl and Good Boy, we did several Nursery Rhymes, all beautifully drawn by Matt, but resolutely and invariably printed only in (frankly rather challenging) *black*, in a continued homage to the type of china we hunted out in antique shops. These Nursery Rhymes designs, When Little Hen, Pussy Cat Pussy Cat and Run Rabbit Run, were among the very last designs produced at Roffenmark, whose stock in trade was copperplate engraving. The fine detail of such pictures was achieved with slow, painstaking skill, tragically accompanied for some of the engravers by the high risk of lung damage from inhaling the tiny filings.

When Matt and I were engaged we discovered that we felt the same about Stephen Long's magical shop, so to my mum's faint annoyance we had a wedding list there. Well, more a few guidelines than a list, really. I remember asking Stephen if this would be hugely inconvenient, and he was as ever unruffled, saying that it had happened before, not much since the 1960s, but from time to time. And that sometimes, particularly if the car was big and expensive, the wedding list customers would get huffy and swish off to Harrods with a banging of car doors. But he was happy to tell people, if they asked, that we'd really love some of his glasses, or which china was our favourite. There was a lovely pair of brass candlesticks, and some of our friends clubbed together to give us a wonderful collection of cups and saucers in many patterns, others a well-worn red quilt (I have added several patches over the years but it's still going strong), and indeed we acquired a fine collection of Victorian glasses from Stephen's shop. And we too found that some people were put off by this rather vague arrangement, so at Mum's insistence we arranged a second list at the kitchenware emporium of David Mellor. The fact is that when I became engaged, she became suddenly much more like the person she had been when first engaged herself; she shed much of her bohemian lightness and set about organising a simply enormous, momentous party. During the run-up to this party I felt dazed, and from the day we came back from our honeymoon life was a whirl, with the days crammed full of business, doing up a house on the Fulham Road and the swift arrival of Elizabeth, then Kitty ... And suddenly, just five years after our wedding, Mum was gone, into the sad half-life she was left with following a hunting accident, and I feel as if I never thanked her properly for taking all that trouble.

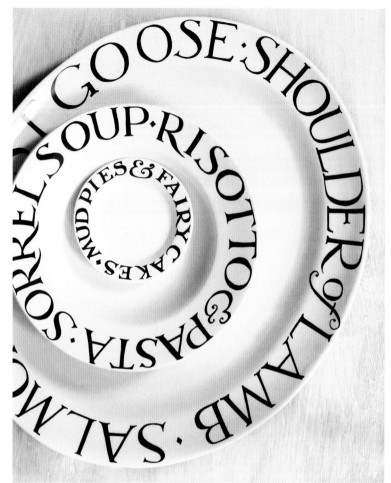

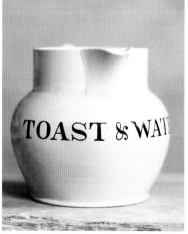

LOVE

LOVE is all you need

In 1994 the Emma Bridgewater catalogue was still dominated by colourful bold spongeware patterns, as much of Matthew's design energy was still focused on his stationery company, Rice Paper, later known simply as Matthew Rice. LOVE was launched then, alongside Knives & Forks, Rose & Border, Marching Elephants, Mermaids and, one of my favourites for its simple repeat and strong colour combination of purple and brown – Cows & Stars. The feel of this group of cheerful patterns fed into the first kitchen textile collection, which came out soon after: LOVE featured on pottery and also on aprons, oven gloves and so on; it was an instant hit. Everyone responded to the directness of the pattern with its scattered letters, whose nice lines are typical of Matthew's dashing calligraphy.

LOVE is all around

At this time we were living in a rented farmhouse in an East Norfolk village: the Worstead years were as happy and uncomplicated as these designs imply and Holly Grove was an easy place to live and to work. Moreover, we had a stream of visits from my younger siblings and cousins, all going through university at the time and nice enough to come for weekends and holidays, often with friends in tow. The swimming pool was in constant use, and there were picnics galore as we explored the Broads and the north-eastern corner of Norfolk, which is wonderfully tucked away and full of secret churches and empty beaches of which Waxham became our favourite. Sometimes I liked to take a full lunch on one of these outings, with say a roast chicken surrounded by veg, still in its tray, and a gooseberry fool in a huge bowl.

Peace, LOVE and understanding

Kerry, who helped out during the week, said to me as we ploughed through an enormous pile of washing one Monday morning: 'Not being funny or anything, but' (always a clue that someone is about to be outspoken, so I braced myself) 'at first we thought you were a cult or something. But now Rocky says you must be in the music business: what are you?' I wasn't really sure how to answer, so I just laughed and said that we are just a very large family. Looking back, I think that most of the excitement was probably caused by my sister Nell, who, along with a horde of friends, had recently shaved off all her hair. She looked completely stunning, in a slightly intimidating way, but some of the others who had succumbed to the clippers looked frankly scary.

Crazy LOVE

The minivan they drove to Norfolk had neither a tax disc, nor a windscreen to stick it on. So I didn't blame Kerry for feeling nosy. And Kerry, along with the rest of the village, was welcoming and friendly: Lizzy, and by this time Kitty too, went to the village school over the road. Our arrival with two school-age children was just in time to keep the school open, and we got on very well with the super-head who was put in to set the school back on track. He encouraged Matt to come and play the piano and teach the children songs, and he even allowed mornings of drilling during which Matt marched the children up and down singing The Grand Old Duke of York. And when our girls had their birthday parties in our garden we invited the whole school (all twenty of them in the first year, but the numbers soon rose). I have never seen such fantastic fancy dress as was dreamed up by all of their families. For Lizzy's Pirate Party, Matt and his friend Nipper built a brilliant assault course which the massed pirates piled over, shouting and yelling. The following year she had a Gypsy Party, with Matt's mum installed in a caravan in full fancy dress as Mystic Pat, telling fortunes. She saw quite a few tall dark handsome strangers approaching, I heard. Yet another year my friend Willy, who is a robust character, started each of the several races (another long obstacle course around the field and garden) with a shot from a 12-bore gun fired into the air. Some said this put his children at an unfair advantage, as most of the candidates were stunned stock-still by the loud bang, while his children shot forward unperturbed.

LOVE LOVE LOVE

The house was rented unfurnished, and although we seemed to have lots of stuff from the sale of Minety, Mum and Rick's house, in fact we lacked all sorts of useful things, which was good, as it gave us a long-running excuse to go to the sales in Aylsham practically every week to buy sofas, bookshelves, kitchen chairs (these always seemed to take heavy casualties, probably because they had already seen a lot of hard wear when they arrived), and there never ever seemed to be enough chests of drawers for all the mothy old clothes. Of course the sales were most diverting, offering bikes, garden tools, books, china, and best of all poultry; Matt almost always came home with boxes and crates of chickens. But I tried to focus on the furniture. And one of the very best acquisitions came not from the sales but was produced by Matthew's father. It was a four-poster bed, much in need of new hangings. And swathes of LOVE fabric were a great solution. Matt tacked these all around, and once made up with mismatched faded seventies sheets of pink and purple, with lots of colourful blankets piled up, well, it was LOVELY.

PRESENTS & CARDS

12 Individual settings :-
* 1/2 pt mug, french bowl 8
cats, Beach, strawb
(Pott set)

1 Creamware vase

2 1st cup : Manchu, Elephants ?
Purple red & Green

3 Dairy :- Butter dish, 1 1/2 pt Jug

7 Wild Strawberries :- Small tea
Sugar pot, 8th botany ring, 6/2

7 Purple stripe :- 4 cup teapot,
(french bowl), 8 1/2" plate, 2td.

4 2 stars : Brown & Purple

F Bathroom : Turquoise coral
3part soap 8x1, Beakers, C

9 Small teapots :-
dove the cove
cats

2 Pasta :- All over in orange's
Salad bowl & Soup plate (

1 Salad :- All over letters & in
Semi, soup dish

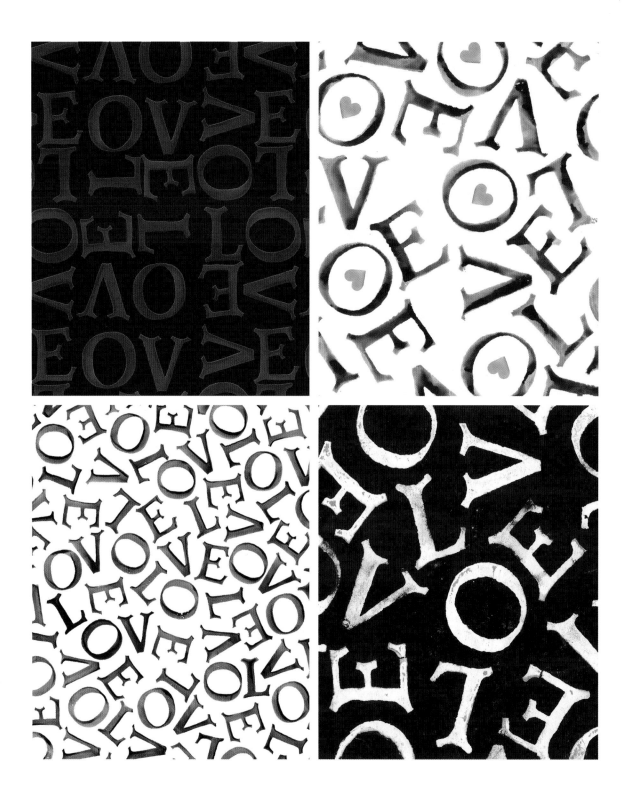

QUEEN OF SHEBA CAKE

This cake is *very* messy – I dare you to take it on a picnic ...
You will need to pack it very skilfully into a snug-fitting cake tin.
It has always been a favourite. Fit for just about all occasions.

Serves 10–12
225g good-quality plain chocolate | 225g butter
4 large free-range eggs | 225g caster sugar | 75g self-raising flour, sifted

To serve
400–500g mixed blueberries and raspberries
2 tablespoons freshly squeezed lemon juice | Caster sugar, to taste
300ml double cream | 2–3 tablespoons finely grated dark chocolate

Preheat the oven to 180°C/160°C Fan/Gas 4. Lightly butter a 20cm round, loose-bottomed cake tin and line with non-stick baking paper.

Break the chocolate into a heatproof bowl and add the butter. Rest the bowl over a pan containing about 3cm of barely simmering water and leave until melted, stirring now and then until smooth. Remove from the pan and leave to cool.

Separate the eggs into two mixing bowls. Beat the yolks with the sugar until pale and thick. Fold in the melted chocolate mixture, followed by the flour.

Whisk the egg whites into soft peaks and gently fold into the chocolate mixture. Pour the mixture into the prepared tin and bake for 45 minutes, or until the cake is just firm, but a skewer, inserted into the centre, still comes away slightly wet. Cover the top with a sheet of brown paper during baking, once it is nicely browned.

Remove the cake from the oven and leave to cool. Then take it out of the tin, pull away the paper and place it on a serving plate.

Put the berries into a serving bowl, stir in the lemon juice and sugar and leave for a few minutes, until the juices start to run. Lightly whip the double cream, spread it thickly over the top of the cake, and sprinkle with the grated chocolate.

Rise & Shine

Now it is a truth universally acknowledged that Matthew is a great expert on *hens*. But I want to put it on record, if we are to talk of these matters (again), that I did know a little bit (a very little, I admit) about poultry-keeping before I met him. I was not what might be called a real hen-wife, and I didn't keep them to sell their eggs as my pocket money, nothing so enterprising, but I grew up with bantams, who kept company with a flock of white fantail pigeons which we fed at the kitchen door, so they were always hanging about on the paving stones right there while I taught myself to skip. And most of Mum's family had similar arrangements, because, as I mentioned elsewhere, my great-grandmother is rumoured to have brought home with her from India a troupe of jungle fowl, exactly like the sort known to breeders now as black/red Indian game. I was thrilled to see actual examples of these very birds, dashing into the undergrowth, when I was in the jungle, in Karnataka, in India. All the family bantams are said to be descended from her little flock. Seeing them in the bushes at Kabini seemed to make the legend slightly more plausible.

> We are reviving this happy combination of chickens,
> and a text about eggs and breakfast, in 2016 because
> these are two of my very favourite themes.

It was the wild characteristics of their bantams that always recommended them to my various aunts and cousins; for once they believe that your garden is their home you need never bother about locking them up again. There is no dreary scraping of poo-crusted roosts, no veterinary attention needed for disgusting health failures; they simply look after themselves, roosting in trees and keeping well out of the way of wayward visiting dogs. The only tricky bit is finding their eggs, but as they lay prodigiously, and they are not very bright, you soon get the hang of their preferred nesting places. Ours are especially keen on the tool bench in one of the barns, where a box of nails is fought over as a top spot to set up a family.

Even if I hadn't been married to Matt I might well have kept a few banties, but thanks to him I often have hundreds instead, and all sorts of larger, more demanding hens as well. Anyway, there they are, always good for modelling a design, and this is what you see on Rise & Shine, a breakfast set which we designed in 2004; it has pale blue Toast script, decorated with beautifully painted bantams who wander in and out of the text – it is perfect for breakfast eggs.

So, how do you like your eggs? Matt likes his fried in butter, with the butter spooned over to cook it through, and a nice curly brown frill; Mikey likes his easy over, and Lil likes hers poached. To make this work, just in case you are not sure, you bring the water to the boil, having dropped in a splash of vinegar and a spoon of salt, while you crack your egg carefully into a cup (if you break the yolk, start again – the fresher the egg the better it hangs together). When the water is boiling, take it off the heat, stir until you have a whirlpool, then tip your egg into the vortex. Lower the heat right down and simmer for two minutes, a little longer for large eggs. Fish the poached egg out with a slotted spoon, roll it carefully on to a tea towel (clean, obvs), and then, having patted away all trace of water, roll the egg on to the buttered toast. Whew!

A performance, yes, but worth it. Margy and Kitty won't touch them (vegetarians both, such a good tease), and I am a bit queasy, maybe due to an awful incident involving a cake and an exploding, rotten egg, so I like mine scrambled, as it seems to make them just a bit less, well, eggy.

And if you thought I made a bit of a thing about poaching an egg, well, you haven't heard my routine for scrambling – it nearly requires me to put on tap shoes and a top hat ... So get ready. Melt an ounce of butter in your heaviest small saucepan. Then when no one is looking, put in another huge lump of butter. And I'd recommend that you stick to fancy butter – have you got any from Normandy? If not, I approve of the local farmhouse type. Danish is minimum spec – if you are still buying cheap imported stuff, stop doing that. Melt this without even slightly browning it. Meanwhile beat your eggs (don't ask me how many, use your initiative) in a generous bowl with a large silver fork until they are completely without trace of yucky separate bits. Now beat some more. I mean it. Take the melted butter off the heat and pour the egg mixture in very slowly and carefully. No, I have not forgotten the salt and pepper, you don't add them until the eggs are on your own piece of toast, OK? Now concentrate, and stir those eggs extremely slowly and gently over the lowest flame while you dexterously toast some thin slices of home-made brown bread. Have someone butter the toast while you keep stirring the eggs. When they are the right consistency, take them off the heat and immediately spoon them on to the toast: some slightly disgusting people like their eggs runny, so serve them first, and so on. I like mine from the bottom of the pan, cooked but not hard. In the unlikely event that you follow these instructions, to the *letter*, you will, I promise, really like the results. So much that you might want to marry me. But then, if I wasn't married to Matt I couldn't guarantee a year-round egg supply, so perhaps it's better if I stick with him.

In our house we also like pancakes, mostly because if supplies are low, with no bread available, not even a stale crumpet, I can almost always rustle up one egg, even if I have to search through all the hardware in the shed, and if I whisk that up with a hillock of flour (absolutely any kind of flour will make perfectly good pancakes) and enough milk to make a batter the consistency of single cream, while melting a knob of butter in a very heavy frying pan, we'll all be piling into the pancakes any minute now. My favourite additions to a pancake are lemon juice and a sprinkle of vanilla sugar. Some swear by maple syrup. Mikey does messy things with Nutella, and Matt would much rather not have pancakes, he'd like sausages, bacon and two fried eggs, but the point is, we are all very lucky, and spoilt even, but we can't always have exactly what we want, now can we?

Peace & Love

This pattern dates from 2005, and came out at the same time as Hearts & Flowers. Bright Flowers followed in 2006. It felt interesting to think about the music of the Incredible String Band, Creedence Clearwater Revival, Janis Joplin, Cat Stevens and all the California hippies whose music was such a memorable element in the soundtrack of my childhood. I wanted to try to evoke the spirit of that tempestuous time, both the idealism of the 60s, and the following slide into industrial unrest and financial downturn. The 70s are regarded as dark and dangerous by contemporary commentators, but nevertheless the music still seems to capture the mood of a much less complicated era than the present. Jesse Winchester is another singer from this time; he, like many young men of his generation, fled to Canada to dodge the draft so as not to have to fight in the Vietnam war. He seems to have been beset with guilt, spending the war years writing romantic regretful songs; he and the rest of these runaways were widely reviled and harshly criticised – rightly so, I guess, though had he declared it, conscientious objection should be seen as extremely brave, surely? Those draft-dodgers were regarded as a shame to society, their behaviour unfathomable; yet compared to the runaways of today, who embrace a militant jihad, throwing themselves into the service of a violent cause, murdering journalists and aid workers on YouTube, the rebels of the early 1970s seem so utterly gentle, so far away and long ago!

Despite the upheaval and unrest of the 1970s I can only think of this time as innocent, probably because it was happening during my own pretty idyllic childhood. In midlife I guess there is a strong tendency to look back with nostalgia, and I'm not the only person doing this, not by a long chalk. Perhaps this is why fashion has a long on-off love affair with a hippy revival. We are certainly just one of many companies producing designs with a feeling for the 70s. That innocence, and also the grainy, grubby cheerfulness of the 70s, is what I love to look back to, when policemen still looked like office workers with comic helmets on top, rather than commandos, and you could jump on and off moving buses if you wanted to chance it as there was little risk management, more of life lived on your own initiative. The telly went off at midnight, when *The Old Grey Whistle Test* ended; and to buy really smutty magazines a chap would have to trudge to Soho in an obligatory flasher's mac, and hand his money over – there was no internet anonymity. I can't help being aware, over and over, of the contrasts between 2005 and 1975, and finding that many of the comparisons give me a pang of longing. Not that last one, well, not personally. But it did make for a simpler time.

Children's parties were home-made affairs – so much weirder, wilder, and so much more fun before we got the ramped-up habit of competitive provision of expensive franchised entertainment. For my younger sisters' parties my friends and I improvised all kinds of strange messy games; one Hallowe'en we fantasised a ghost train experience, rather too successfully scary for its own good. While the squeaking partygoers shuffled around my darkened bedroom, one of the creative team, maybe Choss from number 4, intoned a scary story about grave-yards, body snatchers and ghosts, while we passed them a series of horrid things, such as peeled grapes (*eyeballs!*), a warm peeled tomato (a *kidney!*), a rubber glove full of water tied at the wrist (a rotting *hand!*), some mushrooms (*fungus!*), also hard-boiled eggs (so disgusting I have forgotten what they were!), until, over-come with horror, excitement and tartrazine, our victims hurled the terrifying body parts to the floor and broke for the door, trampling eggs deep into the coco-nut matting. Mum made me scrub the carpet, but the egg never really came out.

Not all the games were scary and messy; most were just messy. My favourite was when we hung doughnuts from the pulley in the kitchen, and set up races, in heats, to see who could eat one completely, in the fastest time, with their hands behind their back. If you made it to the finals you might have eaten three already, so by the end your hair was matted with jam and sugar. Yum. There was a tea towel in the Peace & Love range, it said Peace & Love & Domestic Harmony. That was a rewrite: the first draft read Peace & Love & Domestic Squalor. I guess kitchens got cleaner between 1975 and 2005.

When they were small, I cut my children's hair myself, and despite their extreme lack of cooperation I got quite good at it, but good or not, I cherish the look of Lil and Kitty wearing their village school uniform of gymslips from Woolworths and Barbie T-shirts along with their home-made haircuts. Simply because it looks so much like the photographs of children in the 70s. But almost all their friends went to hairdressers, and soon so did they, and while I encour-aged them to customise their clothes, the pervasive influence of Gap and a thousand other high-street clothes shops had already quite obliterated dress-making at home, so we all look much more like each other now than we did in the photographs of my childhood, *way* back in the past.

So it's an eternal trope, it's what we all feel as we hit middle age, it's one of the first things that the ancients were moved to record for posterity: things just aren't what they used to be. Alas, we are all going to hell in a handcart. So of course it must always be true. Or is it?

I think our tendency towards a wistful conviction that the world of our own childhood was a far, far better place than the present is just an inevitable consequence of the passing of time. When it's gone, it's gone for good, and as you raise your family you try in vain to re-create what seems so vital about your own early experience, but you simply can't go backwards. The smell of a coal fire, now only rarely encountered, perhaps only if you break down on a winter night in County Durham, is so powerfully nostalgic that it ignites in me a rage to pull out the radiators, to shove the grates back into the fireplaces, to drag the coal man out of retirement (and the rag and bone man too, while we are about it, and he can bring his horse), and light a fire in the sitting-room. Right now. But changes propel you ever along with the tide, and unless you are a real off-the-grid eccentric, by now you probably have underfloor heating with digital controls so you can turn up the thermostat from the station car park, and you'll never smell a coal fire on a frosty night, ever again.

The Complete
Emma Bridgewater Pattern Index

This index comes with several health warnings!! We have toiled over our records for weeks, but still I cannot guarantee 100% accuracy. This is intended as a complete round-up of all the patterns which have made it into our catalogues: there are hundreds more which are NOT shown here, including samples, retail specials only sold in our shops or on our website, designs commissioned by other retailers, sale designs and collectors' exclusive designs.

Each pattern is shown alongside the year during which it was introduced, but the withdrawal date is not given: some patterns were very short-lived, while others have lasted for years.

Recently we have used the name Year in the Country as an umbrella for all Matthew's Bird, Flower and Animal designs as they look good displayed together and needed to stand as a group. We have listed Year in the Country (YITC) designs separately, including the early ones, which were not known as such at the time.

Do please let us know via our website if (when?!) you find a missing design ...

1985 ›

4 shapes
Chestnut Leaves

4 shapes
Stipple

4 shapes
Bows

4 shapes
Bows and Teeth

4 shapes
Daffodils

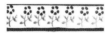

4 shapes
Two Part Flower

4 shapes
Tulip Vase

4 shapes
Cross and Spot

4 shapes
Motifs and Bands

Jug
Gravy, Jugs

Dish
Prawns

Up to 16 shapes
Farmyard

Up to 16 shapes
Pink Tulips

Up to 16 shapes
Fish & Seaweed

Up to 16 shapes
**Hunting: Pigeon,
Rabbit, Lurcher**

Up to 16 shapes
Chintz (3 colourways)

Up to 16 shapes
**Stipple: blue-green, blue,
red. Including Milk, Cream**

Up to 16 shapes
Beach

Up to 16 shapes
Coral

Up to 16 shapes
Rose and Chequers

Up to 16 shapes
Quails

Up to 16 shapes
Noughts and Crosses

Up to 16 shapes
Holly, Christmas Trees

Up to 16 shapes
Pasta, Salad, Fruit

Up to 16 shapes
Butterflies

Up to 16 shapes
Poppies and Corn

Up to 16 shapes
Strawberries

Up to 16 shapes
Trellis and Bows

Up to 16 shapes
Stars and Bands

4 shapes
**Good Boy, Good Girl:
Teddies: red, blue**

1986 ›

Up to 16 shapes
Apricots

Up to 16 shapes
Splatter: blue, pink

Various
**Royal Wedding
(Duke and Duchess of York)**

1987 ›

Up to 19 shapes
Fig

Up to 19 shapes
Striped Tulips

Up to 19 shapes
Sprig and Spot
(2 colourways)

Up to 19 shapes
Birds and Berries

Up to 19 shapes
Rose Border

Nursery
Rabbits

1988 ›

21 shapes
Vine

21 shapes
Vegetable Border

21 shapes
Blue Pomegranate

Breakfast Set
Black Cockerel and Hens

21 shapes
Vegetables

5 shapes
Good Girl: Basket
Good Boy: Boat

1989 ›

Breakfast Set
Morning Glory

Tableware and Tea Set
Waterfield: Wild Plum, Willow,
Tufted Vetch, Blue Cornflower,
Sea Lavender, Sloes (sponged)

Mug
Blackbird with initial

1990 ›

23 shapes
Olives

23 shapes
Lilies
(2 colourways)

5 shapes
Blue House

Breakfast Set
Oranges and Lemons

5 shapes
**Circles, Bird and Flower,
Border and Flower
(not shown)**

12 shapes
**Coloured Glaze:
purple, blue, yellow**

4 shapes
**Dollies' Tea Set:
Tiny Star, Tiny Rose**

3 shapes
**Nursery Rhymes:
Run Rabbit, When
Little Hen, Pussy Cat**

3 shapes
Dairy

1991 ›

Mug
Stars, Polos

Mug
Cherries

Mug
Boats, Traffic

Mug
**Cats, Whippets, Bunnies,
Chickens**

Dish
Good Dog

Mug
For a Friend, Thank You

Platter
Turkey

1992 ›

7 shapes
Toast & Marmalade

16 shapes
Hawthorn
(hand painted)

16 shapes
Black Salmon
(hand painted)

16 shapes
Plums: pink, purple
(hand painted, previously
Waterfield)

Dish
Seafood

Mug
Bless This House

Mug
For My Dearest

Mug
Mother

1993 ›

8 shapes
Knives & Forks

10 shapes
Animals Parade

9 shapes
Marching Elephants

8 shapes
Black Spongeware

7 shapes
**Mermaids and Anchors,
Sea Horses**

Mug
**Crocodile,
Dinosaurs, Frogs**

Mug
**Diggers, Planes,
Cars, Boats**

Mug
**Hippopotamus,
Rhinoceros, Elephant**

5 shapes
**Good Girl, Good Boy:
Traditional Toys**

1994 ›

21 shapes
LOVE

Breakfast Set (3 shapes)
**Strawberry Border, Rose and
Check, Tractors, Butterflies,
Cats, Beach, Stars**

5 shapes
Dollies' Tea Set: Toy Town

Cup and Saucer
Rise & Shine (sponged)

Dishes
Pasta, Fruit, Salad, Seafood

2 shapes
Cows and Stars

3 shapes
**Good Girl: Flower Pots
Good Boy: Teddies and Kites**

Mug
**Dinosaurs, Tractors,
Cars, Elephants**

3 shapes
My First Mug, Bowl, Plate

4 shapes
**Creamware
candlesticks and vase**

1995 ›

18 shapes
Sweet Pea

7 shapes
Purple Stripe

5 shapes
Wild Strawberry

Mug
Copperplate

Serving Bowl
SALAD

Mug
Roman Spongeware
(5 colours)

Mug
**Animal Borders: Pigs,
Chickens, Cats**

Coffee cups and saucers
Indian Spongeware
(6 colours)

2 cup Teapot
Love the Giver

2 shapes
Pasta Shapes

Mug
BOY, GIRL

2 pint jar
Brown stipple

3 shapes
BREAKFAST

1996 ›

12 shapes
Kettle

19 shapes
Red Flower

Teapot, Tea cup
Drink More Tea

Mug
**Aga Saga: brown,
purple, green, red**

Mug
**Violet, Primula,
Nasturtium (not shown)**

Mug
**Circus, Gypsy Camp,
Farm**

Mug
**Chickens, Birds,
Rabbits, Ducks**

Mug
**Wildfowl, Deer,
Boats, Farming**

Mug
Tea, Coffee, Cooking

1997 ›

17 shapes
Toast & Marmalade: blue

12 shapes
Utility

12 shapes
Blue Star

12 shapes
Flower and Star

12 shapes
Blackberry

12 shapes
Working Elephants

8 shapes
Bird & Worm

Mug
**Fruit (3 colourways,),
Pineapple (shown)**

Mug
Blue Hen

Mug
Snowflakes: green, blue, red

Mug
Cows, Sheep, Pigs, Hens

Mug
**Blue Hawking (shown),
Shooting**

Mug
**Daisy: purple, pink
Sunflower, Artichoke**

1998 ›

12 shapes
Blue Hen

17 shapes
Egg and Dart: orange, blue

9 shapes
Holly Sprig

Mug
**Paisley, Seaside,
Pottery (not shown)**
(3 colourways each)

Mug
Cross-Stitch: 4 designs

Mug
Initial

Mug
**Hens, Pigs, Cows: red,
blue, green**

4 shapes
**Schnauzer, Labrador,
Spaniel, Black Cat, Fat Cat**

Mug
Lotus: red, purple

Mug
Clover

6 shapes
**Dollies' Tea Set:
Bird & Worm: blue**

3 shapes
**Good Girl: Outfit
Good Boy: Camping**

1999 ›

31 shapes
**Toast & Marmalade:
Cambridge blue**

5 shapes
Rosehip

7 shapes
Blue Shells

6 shapes
**Dollies' Tea Set:
Tiny Toast & Marmalade**

Cake plate
**Big Ducks, Hens,
Pigs, Cows**

3 shapes
**Blue Pigs, Cows,
Ducks, Frogs**

Mug
**Big Primrose: red (shown),
purple, yellow**

Mug
**Whippet and Garland
(shown), Owl and Garland,
Urn and Garland**

Mug
**Ivy (shown), Tulips,
Honeysuckle, Butterflies**

Mug
**Goose, Hen, Pheasant,
Cock (and border)**

Mug
**Pigeon (shown), Goose,
Guinea Fowl**

3 shapes
**Good Girl: Ark
Good Boy: Train Set**

3 shapes
**Hickety, Baa Baa,
Bye Baby**

Cake plate, 1 pint Mug
Millennium

Mug
Coffee, Tea

2000 ›

15 shapes
Hellebore

9 shapes
Pink Ribbon

3 shapes
Black Glaze

4 shapes
**Cat and Clover,
Dog and Clover**

Dish
**Greens (shown), Pasta,
Salad, Fruit**

8˝ plate
**Birds: Goldfinch, Swallow,
Chaffinch, Song Thrush**
(see YITC index page 280)

4 shapes
Pink Glaze

2 shapes
Eat, Eat, Eat

Cake plate
**Lion
(3 colourways)**

Mug
Dark: Elephant

Mug
**Bright: Elephant,
Butterflies, Indian, Fish
and Weed, Tiny Yellow Rose**

Mug
**Bugs: Damsel Fly, Snail,
Honey Bee**

Mug
**Chickens: Marching,
Broody Coop, Orchard**

Mug
Tulip: yellow, purple, red

Mug
Quilts: Hearts, Star, Chequer

3 shapes
Good Girl: Pink Rose
Good Boy: Roundabout

5 shapes
Dollies' Tea Set:
Tiny Blue Hen

6 shapes
Christmas Toast &
Marmalade

Cake plate
Happy Christmas

2001 ›

9 shapes
Egg and Feather

7 shapes
Stones

4 shapes
Fried Eggs

2 shapes
Chicks and Ducklings
(see YITC index page 280)

Mug
Polka Dot: Happy Birthday

Mug
Seashore: Shrimp,
Crab, Seahorse

Mug
Viola
(2 colourways)

Hen on Nest (small)
Golden Hen on Nest

Mug, candles
Snowflake

Mug
Pencils: Good Luck,
Thank You Teacher

Mug
Polka Star: Thank You

3 shapes
Good Boy: Instruments
Good Girl: Sweeties

2002 ›

14 shapes
Polka Dots

4 shapes, candles
Love & Kisses:
Pink Toast & Marmalade

7 shapes
Rose

21 shapes
Grape

4 shapes
Old English

Coffee cups, saucers
Bright Toast & Marmalade
(4 colours)

3 shapes
Tea Time Toast & Marmalade

2 shapes
Cupcakes

3 shapes
Little Feet

3 shapes
Mud Pies and Fairy Cakes

Mug
Red Star

Mug
Pink Hearts

Mug
Star and Stripe
(USA only)

Mug
Small Flowers:
Forget-me-not, Little Violets

Mug
Small Fruits: Currants
(shown), Pear

Mug
Polka Stripe

Mug
Mother

Mug
Hey Cowboy, Rodeo Girl,
Black Cows, Cow Hide

Mug
Noah's Ark, Doll's House

Mug
Nice Things: Kitchen Shelf,
Dresser Shelf

Mug
Boats and Tractors

Mug
Marching Animals:
Zoo Animals, Farm Animals,
Chickens

2003 ›

5 shapes
Pink Hearts

10 shapes
Red Anemone

6 shapes
Circus

5 shapes
Winter Stars

Mug
Green Hellebore (shown),
Blue Anemone

Mug
Teddy, Lady Bear

Mug
Dumper Trucks, Tractor

Mug
Fireworks

2004 ›

8 shapes
Starry Skies

12 shapes
Starry Toast & Marmalade

8 shapes
Starry Hens

10 shapes
Vegetables
(reworked)

8 shapes
Organic and Green

9 shapes
Clover

6 shapes
Rise & Shine
(litho)

Mug
Woods and Fields
(see YITC index page 280)

4 shapes
Pony, Tractor

Mug, candle
Blue Hearts: Dad

7 shapes
Friends and Parties

2005 ›

7 shapes
Summertime Tulips

6 shapes
Hearts and Flowers
(4 colours)

6 shapes
Blue Hearts

5 shapes
Peace & Love

5 shapes
Coffee and Beans

3 shapes
Blue Animals: Cockerel
(shown), Fox, Hare, Duck

6 shapes
Chatty Penguins

4 shapes
Ducklings Are Fluffy
(see YITC index page 280)

4 shapes
Men at Work

3 shapes
Robin and Berries

2006 ›

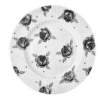

11 shapes
Scattered Rose

3 shapes
Speckled Hen

3 shapes
Polka Dot: red and blue

7 shapes
Bright Flowers

3 shapes
**F is for Fairy,
C is for Cowboy (shown)**

4 shapes
Charm Bracelet

4 shapes
Polka Dot Cockerel

2 shapes and mini mugs
**ABC Alphabet,
Alphabet: A–Z**

Mug
Royal Birthday

Mug
Union Flag
(often incorrectly
named Union Jack!)

Mug
John Betjeman

Mug
Robbie Williams

Mug
**Red Animals: Hare,
Cockerel, Fox**

Mug
Hearts and Pigs

11 shapes
Big Holly

2007 ›

7 shapes
Chicken Run

7 shapes
Kitchen Garden

8 shapes
Holly and Ivy

3 shapes
Dinosaurs

3 shapes
Dancing Mice

3 shapes
Circus

Mug
Polka Hearts

Mug
**I Love My Car: Mini,
Capri, Beetle (not shown)**

2008 ›

8 shapes
Pumpkin

Mug
**Kitty's Christmas:
Stars (shown), Stripes**

Mini mug candle
**Pink Hearts Coordinates:
Stars, Stripes**

Mug
Happiness

Bowl
Pussy Cat

2009 ›

9 shapes
White Toast & Marmalade

6 shapes
Christmas Star

4 shapes
Gymkhana

Mug
Nice Dream: pink, blue

6 shapes
British Birds

2010 ›

8 shapes
Flowers
(see YITC index pages 281–283)

7 shapes
Auricula

Mug
**Pale Toast & Marmalade:
blue, green glazes**

8 shapes
Winter Flowers
(see YITC index pages 281–282)

Mug
Silver Toast & Marmalade

Mug
Union Flag: silver

2011 ›

8 shapes
Sampler

8 shapes
Copperplate

9 shapes
Red Star

2 shapes
Reindeer in a Snowstorm

11 shapes
Joy

6 shapes
Great Britain

Mug
Flying Birds
(see YITC index page 281)

Mug
Buildings:
6 London Buildings
(see YITC index page 281)

3 shapes
Royal Wedding (Prince William and Catherine Middleton) (sponged and litho)

Mug
Polka Dot: blue, green (shown), yellow outer glaze

Mug
Mother's Day, Father's Day

Mug
County Stipple

Mug
Peaches in the Summertime

Mug
Pat Albeck: Butterfly, Pigeon (shown)

Mug
I Dig Dad (shown), Daddy, Best Dad

Mug
LOVE: red

Mug
Big Love: red, blue

Mug
Fabulous Kitchen (3 designs)

2012 ›

5 shapes
Pink Lustre

8 shapes
Walk in the Park

3 shapes
Happiness is a: Pony, Bunny Rabbit
(see YITC index page 282)

7 shapes
Diamond Jubilee
(sponged and litho)

3 shapes
Sampler: Blue, Easter Hen

Mug
Flotilla

Mug
Sporting London, Colourful London, Wonderful London

Mug
Factory Plan

Mug
Red Rooster

Mug
Mum Knows Best

Mug
Romeo and Juliet

Mug
**Sampler: Valentine,
My Darling Mum**

Mug
**Black Toast & Marmalade:
Labrador, Whippet**

2013 ›

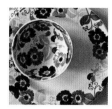

9 shapes
Zinnia

4 shapes
Marmalade

3 shapes
Skyline

6 shapes
**I Love Chocolate, Mum
is Queen, Dad is King**

5 shapes
Splatter

4 shapes
**Wallpaper: Black (shown),
Blue**

2 shapes
Daisy Spot: Blue, Lavender

4 shapes
**Coronation
(60th anniversary)**
(litho and sponged)

2 shapes
Polka Pansy

2 shapes
Petrol Lustre

4 shapes
Pink Eggs

2 Handled Mug
Love & Friendship

Mug
Royal Baby: Prince George

Mug
Cowboys and Cowgirls

3 shapes
Alphabet: pink, blue

3 shapes
**Beatrix Potter:
Peter Rabbit, Flopsy**

16 shapes
Christmas Town

2014 ›

7 shapes
Rose and Bee

9 shapes
Blue Hen and Border

8 shapes
**Pink Wallpaper:
Mum, Be Mine**

Platter, boxed 8″ plates
**Shellfish/Fish: Lobster,
Crab, Shrimp, Prawns,
Langoustine**

2 shapes
Birds and Leaves

6 vases
Badges

4 shapes
Pirates, Mary Mary

Mug
Let's Fall in Love Again

Mug
Sanderson Dresser

10 shapes
Christmas Joy

9 shapes
Christmas Rose

2 shapes
Christmas Stamps

4 shapes
Daisy Spot: green

2015 ›

9 shapes
Folk Border

6 shapes
Purple Veg

5 shapes
Pale Blue Toast & Marmalade

Platter, boxed 8″ plates
Feasting: 9 designs

2 shapes
**Fox and Pheasant:
4 variations**

5 shapes
**Shellfish/Fish: Shellfish,
Fish, Sea Bass, Trout,
Octopus**

3 shapes
Polka Turkey

2 shapes
Owls: 4 variations
(see YITC index pages 282–283)

Mug
**Royal Baby:
Princess Charlotte**

Year in the Country Pattern Index

2000	8" plate	**Garden Birds:** Song Thrush, Goldfinch, Chaffinch, Swallow
	8" plate	**Sea Birds:** Ringed Plover, Oyster Catcher, Puffin, Common Tern
2001	8" plate, Mug	**Ducks:** Teal, Mallard, Pintail, Mandarin
	6" plate, Mug	Chick, Duckling
2002	8 shapes	**Birds:** Robin, Blue Tit
	Mug	**Birds:** Blue Jay, Cardinal (USA only)
	Mug	**Dogs:** Labrador, Whippet
	Mug	**Fish:** Trout, Salmon
	Mug	**Animals:** Cow, Hen, Pig
	4 shapes	**Baby Animals:** Bunny, Frog, Chick, Duckling, Chipmunk (USA only)
2003	Mug	**Birds:** Pheasant, Turtle Dove, Wren, Avocet
	Mug	**Children's:** Penguin
	4 shapes	**Christmas Animals:** Snowy Owl, Deer, Polar Bear
2004	3 shapes	Sparrow
	Mug	**Birds:** Starling, Barn Owl
	Mug	**Woods and Fields:** French Partridge, Grey Partridge
	2 shapes	**Dogs:** Labrador (new drawing), Lurcher, Golden Retriever, Spaniel
	Baby mug	**Dogs:** Dachshund, Labrador puppy, Westie, Terrier
	Mug	**Cats:** Black and White, Ginger Tom, Tabby, Siamese
	Mug	**Kittens:** Black and White, Ginger Tom, Tabby, Siamese
	4 shapes	**Children's:** Lamb
2005	Mug	**Birds:** Long Tailed Tit, Lapwing, Curlew, Bullfinch
	Mug	**Dogs:** Jack Russell, Greyhound
	4 shapes	Ducklings Are Fluffy
	Mug	White Cat
	Mug	**Winter Birds:** Hen Pheasant, Woodcock

2006	*3 shapes*	**Birds:** Great Tit, Black Headed Gull
	Mug	**Birds:** Pied Wagtail, Sandwich Tern
2007	*Mug*	**Birds:** Arctic Tern, Tawny Owl, Little Tern, Bantam Cock
2008	*5 shapes*	British Birds
	Mug	**Birds:** Fieldfare, Golden Plover, Kingfisher, Red Kite
2009	*Mug*	**Birds:** Crested Grebe, Jay, Kestrel, Yellow Hammer, Lapwing in Flight
	Mug	**Spring Flowers:** Snowdrop, Daffodil, Grape Hyacinth, Hellebore, Bluebell, Tulip
	4 cup Teapot	Flowers
	Mug	**Gamebirds:** Pheasant (new), Partridge, Mallard
	Mug	**Christmas Flowers:** Red Hellebore, Ivy, Holly
2010	*Mug*	**Birds:** Bittern, Parakeet, Great Bustard, Golden Oriole, Hoopoe, Waxwing
	Mug	**Dogs** (new drawings): Labrador, Terrier, Lurcher
	Mug	**Flowers:** Auricula, Crocus, Camelia
	6 shapes	Auricula
	6 shapes	Flowers
	Mug	Architectural Primer
	Mug	Year In The Country
	Mug	**Gamebirds:** Snipe, Red Grouse, Blackcock
	3 shapes	Gamebirds
	6 shapes	Winter Flowers
2011	*Mug*	**Birds:** Godwit, Flying Swallows, Canada Goose, Puffin (new), House Martin, Shelduck
	Mug	Flying Birds
	Mug	**Dogs:** Border Terrier, Cocker Spaniel, Golden Labrador, Pug, Chocolate Labrador
	Mug	**Flowers:** Daisy, Rose, Lily, Crocosmia, Nasturtium, Cosmos, Sunflower, Pansy, Morning Glory
	Mug	**Hens:** Lavender Pekin, Speckled Sussex, Cuckoo Maran
	3 shapes	Easter
	Mug	**Buildings:** 6 London Buildings
	Mug	Summer In The Country

Mug	Year In The Country	
Mug	**Christmas (new):** Robin, Pheasant	

2012

Mug	**Birds:** Woodpecker (new), Green Woodpecker, Blackbird, Great Tit, London Pigeon, Mistle Thrush, Nightingale, Nuthatch
Mug	**Dogs:** Beagle, Staffordshire Bull Terrier, Alsatian
Mug	**Flowers:** Zinnia, Primula
Mug	**Wild Flowers:** Birdsfoot Trefoil, Scarlett Pimpernel, Scabious
Mug	**Hens:** Legbar, Buff Orpington, Hamburgh, Wyandotte, Poland, Rhode Island Red
Mug	**Animals:** Red Fox, Red Squirrel, Hedgehog
Mug	Summer In The Country
Mug	Year In The Country
3 shapes	Happiness is a Pony, Bunny Rabbit

2013

Mug	**Birds:** Tufted Duck, Barnacle Goose, Bullfinch
Mug	**Dogs:** Cocker Spaniel, Norfolk Terrier
Mug	**Flowers:** Dahlia, Narcissus
Mug	**Flowers (new):** Snowdrop, Marigold, Daffodil, Tulip
Mug	**Hens:** Light Sussex, Gold Sebright, Hamburgh Red (silver spangled)
Mug	**Animals:** Otter, Hare, Badger
Mug	Easter
Mug	**Gamebirds (boxed):** Grey Partridge (new), Pheasant
Mug	**Owls (boxed):** Little Owl, Barn Owl
Mug	Winter Scene

2014

Mug	**Birds (new):** Goldfinch, Great Tit, Kingfisher, Chaffinch, Turtle Dove
Mug	**Dogs:** Yellow Labrador, Border Collie, Terrier (new drawing)
Mug	**Animals (boxed):** Hedgehog (new drawing), Hare
Mug	**Animals:** Grey Squirrel, Rabbit
Mug	**Hens (boxed):** Dorking, Welsummer
Mug	Halloween
Mug	Easter
Mug	Seaside Landscape, Chicken Landscape
Mug	Cooking, Summer, Gardener, Chickens, Mum, Dad
Mug	**Owls (boxed):** Tawny Owl (new), Snowy Owl (new)
Mug	**Winter Flowers (boxed):** Hellebore (new), Holly
Mug	Winter Scene

2015	*Mug*	**Birds:** Greylag Goose, Barnacle Goose (new)
	Mug	**Seabirds (boxed):** Herring Gull, Arctic Tern (new)
	Mug	**Dogs:** Schnauzer
	Mug	**Dogs (boxed):** 2 Terriers (new)
	Mug	**Dogs (boxed):** 2 Labradors
	Mug	**Flowers:** 2 Tulips (new)
	Mug	**Hens (boxed):** Rise & Shine Hen, All Over Hen
	Mug	**Animals:** Field Mouse
	Mug	**Cats on Rugs:** Black and White, Silver Tabby, Siamese
	Mug	Halloween
	Mug	Winter Scene
	2 shapes	**Owls (boxed):** 4 variations

Recipe List

Acknowledgements

So much love and so many thank yous are due to the magicians of pattern throughout the company, but let's get detailed about this: in the factory studio Leigh, Will, Rachael, Ashley and Becky do extraordinary things with the raw materials that Matt and I throw at them, usually late and messy; they are mind-readers of infinite sweetness who make sure that it is always a pleasure to walk into their sunny rooms and get down to work. Meanwhile in the Bampton studio Claire works unfalteringly, producing reams of lovely designs. Victoria keeps us all on track, spreading warmth and enthusiasm. Lynsey and Carol use their remarkable skills to ease the new designs into the factory, while Steve and Mick keep order in those decorating departments – and let me tell you this is no mean feat! Which brings me to the most wonderful and gloriously feisty team of women I can imagine, the decorating ladies. In the spongeware workshop I must thank Lisa, Amy Davies, Amy Davenport, Julie, Sarah, Maureen, Angela, Clare, Kate, Lynn, Cher, Adele, Tracey, Sharon P, Joanne, Theresa, Sharon S, Kelly, Kerry, Vicky, Jane, Sharon W and Vanessa. The litho decorators are Claire, Melanie, Lynn, Hayley, Marie, Carol, Joanne, Lorraine, Gillian, Wendy and Amy. Trainees Annette, Rebecca, Jenna, Bethany, Joanne, Jessica Bollington, Emma, Jessica Bridgwood, Ellenor, Kelly, Lisa, Amber, Nikki, Danielle, Charlotte, Stephanie Machin, Stephanie McGuiness, Rachel M, Michelle, Louise, Sam, Georgina, Ali, Gemma, Jasmine, Yvonne, Sarah, Rachel W, Laura and Holly; I'm so glad that you have all joined the company. With special thanks to Suzanne and Lisa for cutting the sponges, and to Julie for banding the mugs so beautifully.

I am so privileged to work with all of you.

Of course not one mug would leave the factory without the rest of the Emma Bridgewater factory team, to all of whom, thank you.

Thanks for this wonderful commission to my exceptional editor, Elizabeth, and to Kate, Annie and Rosie at Saltyard Books who have all been so helpful and diligent. Myfanwy, thank you for lovely design work on the book, and Andrew, you are tireless!

Thanks also to Lucy, Martin, Paul, Rosa, Daniela and Andy in Bampton – you are all invaluable, not forgetting Arthur!

Finally, love and a huge thank you to Matthew, Elizabeth, Kitty, Margaret and Michael.

First published in Great Britain in 2016 by Saltyard Books
An imprint of Hodder & Stoughton
An Hachette UK company

1

ISBN 978 1 444 73494 2
eBook ISBN 978 1 444 73496 6

Book design by This Side
Typeset in Austin, Austin Text and Brown

Food stylist Debbie Major
Copy editor Annie Lee
Proof reader Margaret Gilbey

Printed and bound in Germany by Mohn Media GmbH

Saltyard Books policy is to use papers that are natural, renewable
and recyclable products and made from wood grown in sustainable
forests. The logging and manufacturing processes are expected to
conform to the environmental regulations of the country of origin.

Saltyard Books
Carmelite House
50 Victoria Embankment
London EC4Y ODZ

www.saltyardbooks.co.uk

Emma Bridgewater
made in Stoke-on-Trent
England